DRAMA CLASSICS

HEDDA GABLER

by
Henrik Ibsen

translated and introduced by
Kenneth McLeish

London
NICK HERN BOOKS

www.nickhernbooks.co.uk

A Drama Classic

This translation of *Hedda Gabler* first published in Great Britain
as a paperback original in 1995 by Nick Hern Books Limited,
14 Larden Road, London W3 7ST.

Reprinted 2000, 2001

Copyright in the translation from the Norwegian © 1995
by Kenneth McLeish

Copyright in the Introduction © 1995 Nick Hern Books Ltd

Kenneth McLeish has asserted his moral right to be identified as the
translator of this work

Typeset by Country Setting, Kingsdown, Kent CT14 8ES
Printed by Bath Press, Avon

A CIP catalogue record for this book is available from the British Library

ISBN 1 85459 184 3

Introduction

Henrik Johan Ibsen (1828-1904)

When Ibsen was 23, he was appointed writer-in-residence at the newly-established Norwegian National Theatre in Bergen. Six years later he was made Director of the Norwegian Theatre in Kristiania (now Oslo), a post he held until 1862.

Ibsen found his years in the theatre intensely frustrating. The towns were small and the audiences parochial and frivolous-minded. His own plays at the time were chiefly historical dramas, some in verse, modelled on those of Shakespeare, Schiller and Hugo. In the end the Norwegian Theatre lost its audience, ran out of money, and in 1864, after two years of poverty (aggravated by alcoholism and depression) Ibsen left Norway for Italy and Germany, countries in which he spent the next 27 years.

The first two plays Ibsen wrote in self-imposed exile, the verse dramas *Brand* (1866) and *Peer Gynt* (1867), established his reputation. With characteristic iron will, however, he immediately changed his style. He dropped verse for prose (which was more suitable, he said, for 'serious subjects'), and from 1877 onwards, wrote no more plays on historical or folk-inspired subjects. His subsequent plays (a dozen from *The Pillars of Society*, 1879, to *When We Dead Awaken*, 1899) all dealt with contemporary social or philosophical issues, and were set among the provincial bourgeoisie. They regularly caused scandal, and took time to find favour with critics and the middle-class audiences whose lives and concerns they drama-tised. Other critics (notably Archer and Shaw in Britain) rallied to his cause, and by his sixties (the time of his greatest plays), he had become the grand old man not only of Scandinavian literature but of European theatre in general. The 'problem play' of which he was a pioneer has been a staple theatre genre ever since.

Ibsen returned to Norway in 1891. He wrote four more plays, but in 1901 suffered the first of a series of debilitating strokes, the last of which proved fatal.

Hedda Gabler: **What Happens in the Play**

The action takes place in the new house of Jørgen and Hedda Tesman (née Gabler), the day after they return from a six-month honeymoon. One by one, we meet the main characters. Aunt Julia is a good-hearted spinster who brought up her adored nephew Tesman and is dazzled by his marriage to the sophisticated, slightly terrifying Hedda. Tesman, in love equally with Hedda and scholarship, doesn't notice that she fails to share his enthusiasm for domestic crafts in the fourteenth century, and looks forward to being given a professorship – especially now that his main rival, Ejlert Løvborg, seems to be ruled out because of dissipation. Judge Brack, an old friend of Hedda's who organised the buying and furnishing of the new house, looks forward to a cosy 'triangular' friendship with them now that they're back, one in which he can come and go exactly as he pleases. Hedda, for her part, is already bored to distraction by the domesticity of her marriage, and reacts by irony, sharpness and practical jokes on Aunt Julia and Tesman. However, she rejects Brack's offer of intimacy: she chose to marry Tesman and is prepared to put up with the situation, even at the expense of her own happiness. Despite this, she longs for a life to 'control', to feel responsible for. In the poverty of her situation (both existential and literal – Tesman has not yet begun to earn his professorial salary), she says that she has only one comfort left, her father's old duelling pistols.

Into this situation come two outsiders. Mrs Elvsted, an old schoolfellow of Hedda's, arrives from out of town to find Løvborg, who was her children's tutor until he recently disappeared. She reveals that he is a reformed character, that she has helped him to write a book and that she loves him. Brack announces that Løvborg is a candidate for the same professorship as Tesman, and finally Løvborg himself arrives, to the consternation of both Tesman and Hedda. Tesman is dismayed (though professionally excited) by the brilliance of Løvborg's ideas, particularly those in the book-manuscript he's carrying. Hedda is disturbed by memories of their previous relationship, and by jealousy of his and Mrs Elvsted's intimacy. Even so, when he tries to flirt with her, she spurns him as she previously rejected Brack.

The men go to Brack's for a bachelor party. Mrs Elvsted has tried and failed to stop Løvborg going, and Hedda has urged him to show that he is still in control of his own destiny, and to come back 'with vine leaves in his hair'. The party lasts all night, and when Tesman returns, dishevelled, we learn that it turned into a drunken orgy, and that Løvborg got so drunk that he lost the precious manuscript which he, Tesman, rescued. Tesman gives the manuscript to Hedda to return to Løvborg, and goes to lie down. Hedda, however, has other plans. When Løvborg arrives, distraught by the loss of his book and blaming himself for 'killing his own child' by giving in once more to dissipation, instead of telling him that it's found she gives him a pistol and tells him to salvage his dignity and integrity by making a 'fine' suicide. As soon as he's gone she stuffs the manuscript in the stove and burns it.

When Tesman wakes up, Hedda tells him about the package, and claims that she burned it for his sake and because she's carrying their child. Tesman, overwhelmed by the thoughts that she loves him and that his future is secure, stifles his moral qualms. But then Brack comes in to report that Løvborg is dead – not 'finely', but sordidly after a brawl in a brothel –

and Tesman and Mrs Elvsted decide to reconstruct the book from Løvborg's notes and Mrs Elvsted's memory (Løvborg dictated it to her). Hedda asks if she can help, and they brush her aside. Brack tells her that the police have her pistol, and that he (Brack) will tell them who it belongs to unless she agrees to go on living 'on his terms'. Instead of her controlling another human being's destiny, she has delivered herself into someone else's power. Stripped of everything she once had or used to be, she goes into the next room and shoots herself.

The 'Problem' Play and the 'Well-Made' Play

The 'problem' play was a response, in mid-19th-century European theatre, to an upsurge in public discussion of 'big' social and philosophical issues. Favoured topics were the differing natures and social roles of women and men, family relationships, sexual behaviour, religion, politics and social ethics. The plays were set among ordinary, contemporary people, whose dilemmas onstage embodied the questions under discussion. The 'problem' plays of some writers – for example Bjørnson in Norway, Sardou in France, Grundy and Jones in Britain – were often creaking and contrived: sermons or newspaper leaders disguised as art. (Shaw coined the nickname 'Sardoodledum'; Wilde memorably said, 'There are three rules for the young playwright. The first rule is not to write like Jones. The second and third rules are the same.') But in other hands, notably Ibsen's, concentration on character and on personal tragedy elevated the form. Even such preachy plays as *Ghosts* or *An Enemy of the People* make their impact through the vitality of their characters and situations rather than the underlying issues they address.

Rules for the 'well-made' play were formulated in France in the early 19th century, and quickly spread throughout Europe. They were as strict as those Aristotle laid down for ancient tragedy (see below, p. x). In a 'well-made' play, action should be organised in three sections: exposition of the central problem, alarms and excursions, dénouement. The plot should hinge on a secret or a dilemma which affects the main character; the audience should be allowed only hints and glimpses of this as the play proceeds, and all should be fully revealed only as the action moves towards dénouement. There should be reversal of fortune – 'up' in a 'well-made' farce, 'down' in a 'well-made' melodrama. And finally, settings, dialogue and behaviour should be contemporary and conventional. Tens of thousands of 'well-made' plays were written, and most are justly forgotten. (Victorian melodramas are typical examples.) But in the hands of fine writers – Dumas' *Lady of the Camellias* and Labiche's farces spring to mind, not to mention Maugham's or Rattigan's plays in a later age – the recipe has led to masterpieces. 'Well-made' conventions, in whole or in part, were particularly useful to writers of 'problem plays', whose effect on their audience depended, in part, on putting a spin on familiar-seeming characters and situations and on received ideas.

Hedda Gabler

Hedda Gabler was first produced in 1890. It deals with a favourite Ibsen theme, the conflict between individual spiritual freedom and the claims of convention and society. It resembles the plays which preceded it (*Pillars of the Community*, *A Doll's House*, *Ghosts*, *An Enemy of the People* and *The Wild Duck*) in that it is entirely realistic, tragedy in a domestic setting. (In fact domesticity is one of the main causes of the tragedy.) At the same time, it anticipates some of the symbolism and 'otherness' of such later plays as *Master Builder Solness* or *Rosmersholm*. There are times when it is not just to herself, but to the other characters and to us as well, that Hedda seems to come from a different planet from everyone else. (Ibsen may have had this quality in mind when he talked of the play's 'demonism'.)

Hedda Gabler quickly became established, not least because it offers such a superb challenge to the leading actress. Within a few months of its Norwegian premiere, it was staged in Germany, Britain and the USA, and it has been revived more frequently than any Ibsen play except *The Wild Duck*. (Notable English-language Heddas, over the years, have included Janet Achurch, Mrs Patrick Campbell, Sonia Dresdel, Peggy Ashcroft and Fiona Shaw. In 1975 Glenda Jackson played the role on screen, recreating her striking stage performance.) It has influenced playwrights from Shaw (*Candida* follows its structure particularly closely) to Albee (*Who's Afraid of Virginia Woolf* plays bleak variations on its themes of marital incompatibility and emotional dependence and predation), and its legacy is also apparent in hundreds of excellent film melodramas, from Joan Crawford's and Bette Davis' 1940s vehicles to the more recent, more explicitly feminist 'problem films' of such actresses as Jane Fonda and Meryl Streep.

Form

Ibsen's later plays are formally dazzling: tightly structured, without a loose end or a wasted word. But even among them, *Hedda Gabler* is exceptional. One of the most striking things about it is its harmonisation of the the conventions of the 'well-made' play with a much grander set of 'rules': those deduced from classical Greek tragedy and noted by Aristotle. *Hedda Gabler* observes the unities: it happens in one place, in a single stretch of time, in a sequence of action which proceeds without interruption or divergence from beginning to end. Characters and action are totally integrated: even Aunt Rina, lying unseen on her death-bed, plays a crucial role in the unfolding of events. The plot concerns a 'tragic flaw' in the leading character: a psychological failing, at first unperceived, which is gradually revealed and which engenders the character's doom. That doom is inevitable from the beginning of the play, and is worked out inexorably before our eyes. There is a moment of recognition: a climactic point when the leading character realises that she is trapped by her own nature and actions and that her destruction is inevitable. The cathartic event of violence takes place offstage.

Aristotelian ideas influence the play's structure as well as its themes. The characteristic organisation of structure in surviving Greek tragedy is an introduction and five sections, of which the last is a kind of extended musical 'coda'. These are interspersed with choral sections which link, frame and counterpoint the main action. The five-act division of Renaissance tragedy probably imitated this pattern, without the choruses. In *Hedda Gabler*, Ibsen follows a four-act pattern, dispensing with the coda. Each Act, like each spoken section in Greek tragedy, is a contained thematic unit, advancing the action in a single direction, moving it a few more irretraceable steps towards ultimate catastrophe. The content of Acts 2-4 is not guessable at the end of Act One; that of Acts 3-4 is not guessable at the end of Act Two, and so on – and yet, in retrospect, we recognise that each later event has been prepared and prefigured in what has gone before. The sense of inevitable progression is also achieved by the narrowing focus of the action. Each Act is shorter than the one before, and the broad sweep of the opening (exhibiting Berta's character, for example, for the only time in the play, before revealing something of Hedda's and Tesman's characters in the way they treat Aunt Julia) is never repeated, yielding instead to extremely close attention on single moments, individual relationships, single plot-developments. The way in which, in the play's last three or four pages, Hedda is left with nothing, and with nowhere to turn, is remarkable given that the rhythms of the writing are as easy and everyday as in the entire rest of the play (see page xiii). Its power comes from the inexorable elimination of the inessential, the irising-in, which has preceded it and has continued, uninterrupted, from the first moments of Act One.

Fate and Hubris

Although Ibsen follows the 'rules' of Greek tragedy (so closely that it seems unlikely to be by chance), he studiously avoids one of its major themes. Greek tragedies were part of a religious occasion, and their action – usually drawn from myth – arose from the attempts of human beings to come to terms with the nature and demands of the supernatural. The gods in Greek tragedy are devious, all-powerful and implacable, and the fate they oversee for mortals is arbitrary (at least in mortal eyes) and inescapable. The tragic flaw which destroys the protagonist is often hubris: the arrogance which makes mortals think they can transcend their own mortality. None of this applies in Ibsen. Sternly atheist, unswervingly rationalist, he allows religion no part in the events of *Hedda Gabler*. When characters do invoke God (Tesman; Mrs Elvsted; Miss Tesman) it is a superficial, conventional way of talking, to add emphasis to otherwise bland remarks – and Ibsen the ironist takes it one step further when he makes Brack invoke, for the same purpose, not the deity but the devil. The only 'supernatural' force in *Hedda Gabler* is a bleak certainty that to think is to suffer and to take a moral stand is to die. Two of the most 'religious' characters, Tesman and Mrs Elvsted, are involved in the greatest compromises of principle. This is not Fate but a kind of personification of Ibsen's characteristic pessimism: inevitability of failure seen almost as an enabling force, at least until you fail.

The second main force on Ibsen's characters, as dominating as the power of religious observance in Greek tragedy, is social convention. Society and its rules may be human constructs (but so, Ibsen the atheist might have argued, are religious dogma and ritual); but their weight, in this play, is as great as if they had been ordained by God. Characters may take a dozen different approaches to them, from unthinking observance through ironical lip-service to manipulation and challenge, but the rules themselves seldom change. Given Hedda's 'station' in life, and given the situations of Tesman and his aunts, no

meeting of minds is possible without self-destructive compro-
mise on someone's part. For Tesman (essentially not a 'noble'
character) marriage with Hedda was a gift of chance, a stroke
of luck to be snatched, like some wish in a fairy tale, before it
disappeared. For Hedda (a 'noble' character) marriage with
Tesman was an act of hubris, whose unlikelihood of success
she very well knew before she did it. They, and indeed all
characters in the play, are imprisoned in themselves, each in
what they are – another of Ibsen's commonest, iciest themes.

Language

Throughout *Hedda Gabler*, tightness of form and thematic
concentration are balanced by the extraordinary freedom and
colloquialism of the language. (The stylistic tension this sets up
embodies, in an entirely unforced way, the pull between
Apollonian control and Dionysian abandon which underlies the
plot.) Only Miss Tesman speaks with an old-fashioned, faintly
artificial turn of phrase, as if she were using a language
learned from books or samplers rather than from real life. All
other characters speak brisk, unambiguous prose whose self-
confident slanginess must have fallen like a cold shower on the
ears of Ibsen's first audience. There is no hint of literary
stodginess, of the kind sometimes imparted by translators over-
respectful of Ibsen's status as a 'literary classic'. The language
is intentionally ordinary, and its vernacular simplicity gives
pace, verve, and opportunity for darkly comic points-scoring
and irony. (All characters, even Berta, use irony.)

For all its insouciant appearance, Ibsen handles this continuum
of everyday looseness and naturalness of speech with a virtu-
osity matching his use of form. The rhythms of the dialogue, in
both individual characters' utterances (which reflect the move-
ment, or non-movement, of their minds) and in whole scenes
and acts, is precisely controlled. Early 20th-century critics
somewhat fancifully compared *Hedda Gabler* to a symphony.

Its four acts, they said, like symphonic movements, might differ
in theme and content but were all recognisably part of the
same overall conception, aspects of the same mental landscape.
In fact the musical analogy aids our understanding of the play's
language more than of its form. Ibsen controls pace, for example,
or presents, repeats and varies crucial ideas or turns of phrase,
as a symphonic composer develops musical themes. A simple
example is the by-play between Hedda, Brack, Løvborg and (in
a minor way) Mrs Elvsted on the notions of trust, comradeship
and the need for, and nature of, a single 'beautiful',
existentially self-defining action in each person's life. These
exchanges play with a dozen repeated words, as children might
pick up toys, look at them and pass them from hand to hand.

A more complex example, articulating Ibsen's presentation of
the formality of the society in which the characters move, is
the enormous variety of modes of address employed. In
English we have perhaps a dozen ways of addressing strangers,
acquaintances and intimates. Nineteenth-century Norwegian
had many more, and the nuances were far more scrupulously
noted. Ibsen makes constant use of this, freighting slight
changes of address with emotional and psychological meaning.
Thus, the ways in which Hedda addresses Tesman, Løvborg
and Brack – and the way she varies modes of address almost
from speech to speech – vitally reflect her changing state of
mind and the attitudes she strikes. This happens not just in
obvious places (for example her first scene alone with Løvborg,
where it is almost possible to deduce, from the ways they
address each other, the depth of passion in their relationship
before Hedda's marriage), but also in the apparently bland ebb
and flow of ordinary dialogue. For example, Hedda's changing
feelings about Tesman, and her sense of what she wants from
him, are reflected by what she calls him. A single instance
makes the point: Ibsen's careful placing of the very few
occasions when she calls her husband 'Jørgen'.

Stage Directions

To modern eyes, Ibsen's plays can seem cluttered with unnecessarily explicit stage directions. In particular, his instructions to the actors about how to deliver the lines can seem both pedantic and fustian. Modern conventions, we might argue, are different; we play by our own rules. But it seems at least plausible that Ibsen, so scrupulous about every other kind of artistic effect, might have organised the emotional blocking of each scene with as much care as he did everything else. What we have, in short, may be analogous less to the stage-directions in an 'acting edition' than to the instructions for performing-nuance which composers (again!) write on music. For this reason, the present translation retains all original directions, whether they look over-explicit or not.

Kenneth McLeish, 1995

Thanks to Stephen Mulrine and Stephen Unwin for advice during the preparation of this translation.

For Further Reading

Michael Meyer, *Henrik Ibsen* (three vols, 1967-71; one vol, 1992) is a lively biography, plump with quotations from letters, reviews and other documents, and excellent on the theatrical and political background to Ibsen's life. Its only defect – somewhat heavy-handed literary criticism – is offset by John Northam, *Ibsen: a Critical Study* (1973): a scholarly but readable discussion of themes and techniques of the prose plays. The most recommendable book on Ibsen is the oldest of the three: George Bernard Shaw, *The Quintessence of Ibsenism* (1891). Written by one of Ibsen's first European devotees (anxious to give the master a place in serious drama analogous to Wagner's in music), and with all Shaw's usual tongue-in-cheek self-projection, this book nevertheless balances gush and fervour with remarkably clear-headed intellectual discussion of the 'theatre of ideas' in general and each Ibsen play in particular. Few books examine Ibsen so lucidly and with such creative fellow-feeling; few make a more enthusiastic case.

Ibsen: Key Dates

1828 Born (to well-to-do, bourgeois parents)
1832 Father bankrupt
1843 Apprenticed to an apothecary
1850 Fails university entrance exam; writes first play (*Catiline*)
1851 Playwright-in-residence at National Theatre in Bergen
1857 Appointed Director of Norwegian Theatre, Kristiania
1862 Theatre closed down
1864 Moves to Rome
1866 *Brand*
1867 *Peer Gynt*
1868 Moves to Dresden
1869 *The League of Youth*
1873 *Emperor and Galilean*
1877 *Pillars of the Community*
1879 *A Doll's House*
1881 Returns to Rome; *Ghosts*
1882 *An Enemy of the People*
1884 *The Wild Duck*
1885 Moves to Munich; summer in Norway, first visit since 1864
1886 *Rosmersholm*
1888 *The Lady from the Sea*
1890 *Hedda Gabler*
1891 Returns for good to Norway
1892 *Master Builder Solness*
1894 *Little Eyolf*
1896 *John Gabriel Borkman*
1899 *When We Dead Awaken*
1901 First of several strokes
1906 Dies

HEDDA GABLER

Characters

JØRGEN TESMAN, *a cultural historian*

HEDDA TESMAN, *née Hedda Gabler, his wife*

MISS JULIA TESMAN, *his aunt (Norwegian: Juliane)*

MRS ELVSTED

BRACK, *a circuit judge*

EJLERT LØVBORG

BERTA, *the maid (Norwegian: Berthe)*

The action takes place in Tesman's house in the western part of town. There are four acts.

Pronunciation

Jørgen – like the English word 'Yearn'

Ejlert – EYE-lert ('eye' as in 'eyesight')

Løvborg – LE(R)V-bor (silent 'R')

ACT ONE

A smart, spacious living room, stylishly decorated in dark colours. Upstage, a wide double-doorway, with its curtains drawn back, leads into a smaller room, decorated in the same style. Right, exit to the hall. Opposite left, through a glass screen door with its curtains also drawn back, can be seen part of a raised verandah and a garden. It is autumn. Centre stage, dining chairs and an oval table covered with a cloth. Downstage right, against the wall, a dark tiled stove, a wing chair, an upholstered footstool and two stools. Upstage right, a corner seat and a small table. Downstage left, a little out from the wall, a sofa. Upstage of the screen door, a piano. On either side of the main double-doorway, whatnots displaying artefacts of terracotta and majolica. In the inner room can be seen a sofa, a table and two chairs. Over the sofa hangs the portrait of a handsome elderly man in general's uniform. Over the table, a hanging lamp with a pearled glass shade. All round the main room are vases and glass containers full of cut flowers; other bouquets lie on the tables. Thick carpets in both rooms. Sunlight streams in through the screen door.

Enter MISS JULIA TESMAN *and* BERTA *from the hall.* BERTA *is carrying a bouquet.* MISS TESMAN *is a placid-looking woman of about 65. Her grey outdoor clothes are plain but well-made.* BERTA *is a simple countrywoman, getting on in years.* MISS TESMAN *stops in the doorway and listens.*

MISS TESMAN (*in a low voice*). They *aren't* up yet!

BERTA (*in a low voice*). I told you, Miss Tesman. The boat came in very late last night. And even then, mercy!, the things the young lady had to unpack before she'd go to bed.

MISS TESMAN. We won't disturb them. But we *will* let some air in for when they do get up.

She opens the screen door, wide. BERTA, *at the table, is not sure what to do with her flowers.*

BERTA. There's no room anywhere. I'll put them over here.

She props them on the piano.

MISS TESMAN. Just fancy, Berta – you, and a new mistress. I don't know how I brought myself to part with you.

BERTA (*close to tears*). It was hard for me too, Miss Tesman. After all these years, with you and Miss Rina.

MISS TESMAN. Now, Berta, what else could we do? Jørgen needs you here. Needs you. Ever since he was a little boy, he's relied on you.

BERTA. Oh Miss Tesman, I keep thinking of that poor lady lying at home. Can't do a thing for herself, poor soul. And a new maid now. That one won't learn how to look after an invalid.

MISS TESMAN. I'll show her. And I'll do much more myself. Dear Berta, for my poor sister's sake, don't worry so.

BERTA. There's something else, Miss Tesman. The new mistress . . . I'm afraid . . . I won't give satisfaction.

MISS TESMAN. Don't be silly. There may be a few small difficulties, at first –

BERTA. She's such a particular lady.

MISS TESMAN. Of course she is. General Gabler's daughter. The style she had, when her father was alive! D'you remember her riding beside him, down the road? In that long black skirt? With the feather in her hat?

BERTA. Oh yes, Miss Tesman. I'd never have dreamed, back then, that one day she'd marry Mr Jørgen.

MISS TESMAN. We none of us dreamed it, Berta. But so she did. Oh and Berta, you mustn't call Jørgen 'Mister' any more. He's 'Doctor Tesman' now.

BERTA. The young lady told me that as well, as soon as they got in last night.

MISS TESMAN. Just fancy, Berta, they made him a doctor while he was away. On honeymoon. I didn't know a thing about it, till he told me at the pier last night.

BERTA. Such a clever man. He can do anything he sets his mind to. But even so . . . curing people!

MISS TESMAN. Not that kind of doctor. (*With meaning.*) In any case, before long you may be calling him something else.

BERTA. Miss Tesman, what do you mean?

MISS TESMAN (*with a smile*). Ah! Wait and see. (*With emotion.*) If poor dear Jochum could only come back, and see what's become of his little boy! (*Looking round.*) Berta, what have you . . . ? Why ever have you . . . ? You've uncovered all the furniture.

BERTA. Madam told me. She won't have covers on chairs, she said.

MISS TESMAN. So they'll be using this room, making this their sitting room?

BERTA. So madam said. Mr Jørgen . . . Doctor Tesman . . . he said nothing.

Enter TESMAN *from the inner room, right. He is humming, and carrying an empty, unlocked suitcase. He is 33, fresh-faced, medium height, stoutish. Blonde hair and beard; round, open, happy face. Glasses; casual, almost rumpled clothes.*

MISS TESMAN. Good morning, Jørgen.

TESMAN (*in the doorway*). Aunt Julia! Aunt Julia! (*Shaking her hand.*) Fancy coming all this way, so early. All this way.

MISS TESMAN. I had to see you both, take a good look at you.

TESMAN. You've hardly had time to sleep.

MISS TESMAN. That doesn't matter.

TESMAN. You got home from the pier all right?

MISS TESMAN. Judge Brack was very kind, took me right to the door.

TESMAN. We were so sorry we couldn't give you a lift. But you saw for yourself. The carriage was full. All Hedda's luggage.

MISS TESMAN. Hedda's luggage. Yes.

BERTA (to TESMAN). Shall I go and ask madam if she needs any help?

TESMAN. No, Berta. Thank you. There's no need. She says she'll ring if she wants you.

BERTA (about to go). Yes.

TESMAN. Oh Berta, take this suitcase.

BERTA (taking it). I'll put it in the attic.

Exit through the hall, right.

TESMAN. It was wonderful, Aunt Julia. That whole case, full of notes. You wouldn't believe what I found, going round the museums. Old documents, artefacts, things no one's bothered with before.

MISS TESMAN. Dear Jørgen! You made good use of your honeymoon?

TESMAN. I certainly did. But take your hat off, auntie. Here, I'll unpin it for you.

MISS TESMAN (while he does so). It's as if you were still at home with us.

TESMAN (turning the hat over). What a wonderful hat! Is it new?

MISS TESMAN. I bought it because of Hedda.

TESMAN. Pardon?

MISS TESMAN. So that she won't be embarrassed when we go for walks together.

TESMAN (*patting her cheek*). Aunt Julia, how thoughtful you are!

He puts the hat on a chair by the table.

Sit down, here on the sofa, next to me. Let's have a gossip, till Hedda comes.

They sit. She rests her parasol in the corner of the sofa. She takes his hands and gazes at him.

MISS TESMAN. It's so good to have you home again. Dear Jørgen. Poor Jochum's own little boy.

TESMAN. Dear Aunt Julia. You've been father and mother to me, all these years.

MISS TESMAN. Promise you won't forget your poor old aunties.

TESMAN. How is Aunt Rina? No better?

MISS TESMAN. Oh Jørgen, you know she'll never get better. She's lying there, as she's lain there all this time. Every day I pray the good Lord to spare her for a few years more. If she died, I don't know what I'd do. Especially now, Jørgen, now I don't have you to look after.

TESMAN (*patting her back*). Now, now, now.

MISS TESMAN (*brightening*). Just imagine, we never expected to see Jørgen Tesman married. And to Hedda Gabler, too. Imagine. You, and Hedda. She had so many beaux.

TESMAN (*smiling, humming a little tune*). You're right. Some of my friends must be quite green-eyed. No doubt of it. No doubt.

MISS TESMAN. And such a long honeymoon! Five . . . six months.

TESMAN. I made it a field trip. All those museums. All those books to read.

MISS TESMAN. That's right. (*Lower, more confiding.*) You . . . haven't any other news?

TESMAN. From the honeymoon?

MISS TESMAN. Exactly.

TESMAN. I don't think so. It was all in my letters. My doctorate – I told you that yesterday.

MISS TESMAN. Of course you did. I'm talking about . . . other prospects.

TESMAN. Prospects?

MISS TESMAN. Oh Jørgen, I am your aunt.

TESMAN. Well, of course I've other prospects.

MISS TESMAN. I thought so!

TESMAN. For example, I'm pretty sure that one day I'll be . . . a professor.

MISS TESMAN. A professor.

TESMAN. In fact, not 'pretty sure': really sure. But you know that already, auntie.

MISS TESMAN (*with a light laugh*). That's right. (*Changed tone.*) But we were talking about the honeymoon. It must have cost a fortune.

TESMAN. I did have that grant.

MISS TESMAN. Enough for two? I don't believe it.

TESMAN. Not entirely.

MISS TESMAN. Of course not. Two never travel as cheaply as one. Especially when one of them's a lady. That's what people say.

TESMAN. It's true. But Hedda needed that trip. No question. Needed it.

MISS TESMAN. A honeymoon abroad. That's essential nowadays. Or so they say. Well now, Jørgen, have you had time to look round the house?

TESMAN. I've been up since dawn, exploring.

MISS TESMAN. And what d'you think?

TESMAN. Wonderful! Won-derful! The only thing I can't imagine . . . What will we do with those two empty rooms, between the hall there and Hedda's bedroom?

MISS TESMAN (*with a light laugh*). Oh Jørgen, you'll find a use for them soon. You'll see.

TESMAN. You're right, auntie. After all, I'll need somewhere for my books.

MISS TESMAN. Just what I meant: your books.

TESMAN. I'm pleased most of all for Hedda. Before we were married, she often said she'd never be happy unless she could live in the old Falk villa.

MISS TESMAN. And then it came on the market. While you were away.

TESMAN. So lucky, aunt Julia, so lucky.

MISS TESMAN. But expensive, Jørgen. This will all cost money.

TESMAN (*looking at her, a little downcast*). You think so?

MISS TESMAN. Well, of course it will!

TESMAN. How much do you think? About.

MISS TESMAN. Who knows, till the bills come in?

TESMAN. Thank heavens Judge Brack saw to everything. Made a wonderful bargain. He explained it all to Hedda, in a letter.

MISS TESMAN. No need to worry on that account. And I gave security for the furniture, the carpets.

TESMAN. Aunt Julia, what possible security could you put down?

MISS TESMAN. I mortgaged the annuities.

TESMAN (*jumping up*). Your annuities? Yours and aunt Rina's?

MISS TESMAN. There aren't any others.

TESMAN (*facing her*). Auntie, you're crazy. Those annuities – they're all you and Aunt Rina have to live on.

MISS TESMAN. Don't worry. It was just a formality. His Honour said so. He arranged everything. He told me: a formality.

TESMAN. Maybe. Maybe. But even so . . .

MISS TESMAN. And now you've an income of your own to rely on. In any case, why shouldn't we spend a little . . . to give you a start . . . ? It's a pleasure, Jørgen, a pleasure.

TESMAN. Oh auntie, you're always sacrificing yourself for me.

MISS TESMAN *stands and puts her hands on his shoulders.*

MISS TESMAN. In all the world, what matters more to me than smoothing the path for my darling boy? All these years you've had no mother, no father. And now it's all right. We've reached harbour. Once or twice, the skies looked black. But you managed, Jørgen, you succeeded.

TESMAN. Things certainly have gone well.

MISS TESMAN. Your rivals, the people who blocked your path – you've passed them. They've fallen, Jørgen. And he's fallen furthest of all, the one you'd most to fear. The poor man's made his bed, and now he must lie on it.

TESMAN. How is Ejlert? Have you heard any news? I mean since I went away.

MISS TESMAN. I don't think so. He's published a book.

TESMAN. Ejlert? Recently?

MISS TESMAN. So they say. It's nothing important. Now, when your book comes out, Jørgen, that'll really be something. What's it about?

TESMAN. Domestic crafts in fourteenth-century Brabant.

MISS TESMAN. Fancy being able to write about things like that!

TESMAN. It may take some time. All this new research. I've that to catalogue before I start.

MISS TESMAN. Cataloguing. Research. You're so good at that. You're not Jochum's son for nothing.

TESMAN. I can't wait to start. Especially with such a comfortable home to work in.

MISS TESMAN. Ah Jørgen – and especially now you've the wife you set your heart on.

TESMAN (*hugging her*). Yes, auntie! Hedda. She's the best thing of all.

He looks towards the door.

I think she's coming.

Enter HEDDA *from the inner room left. She is 29, a woman of style and character. Her complexion is smooth and pale; her grey eyes are cold, clear and calm. Attractive, light-brown hair, not particularly full. A modish, loose-fitting morning dress.* MISS TESMAN *goes to greet her.*

MISS TESMAN. Good morning, my dear, good morning.

HEDDA (*shaking her hand*). Miss Tesman, good morning. How kind of you to call so early.

MISS TESMAN (*seeming a little flustered*). I hope you slept well, in your new home.

HEDDA. Fairly well, thank you.

TESMAN (*with a laugh*). Oh Hedda, fairly well! You were sleeping like a log when I got up. A log!

HEDDA. Wasn't that amazing? One gets used to new experiences all the time, Miss Tesman. Gradually. (*Glancing left.*) Look, the maid's left the verandah door wide open. There's a *sea* of sun.

MISS TESMAN (*going to the door*). Why don't we close it, then?

HEDDA. No, no. Tesman, please draw the blinds. A softer light.

TESMAN (*at the door*). There. There. Now you've shade *and* fresh air.

HEDDA. Fresh air, thank goodness. These dreadful flowers. Do sit down, Miss Tesman.

MISS TESMAN. I just came to see that everything's as it should be – and it is, it is. Now I really must hurry. She'll be waiting, lying there, poor soul.

TESMAN. Kiss her from me. Tell her I'll pop round this afternoon.

MISS TESMAN. I'll tell her. Oh, Jørgen, I nearly forgot . . .

She rummages in her bag.

I've something for you.

TESMAN. What, auntie?

MISS TESMAN *gives him a flat wrapped package.*

MISS TESMAN. What d'you say to this?

TESMAN (*opening it*). You kept them! Look, Hedda. Isn't this wonderful?

HEDDA (*at the whatnot upstage right*). Yes. What?

TESMAN. My slippers. Look!

HEDDA. The ones you kept talking about while we were away.

TESMAN. I really missed them.

He goes to her.

Now you can see them in person!

HEDDA *crosses to the stove.*

HEDDA. There's really no need.

TESMAN (*going after her*). Aunt Rina embroidered them with her own hands. Lying there. That poor invalid. You can imagine the memories in every stitch.

HEDDA (*by the table*). No memories for me.

MISS TESMAN. Hedda's right, Jørgen.

TESMAN. But now she's one of the family –

HEDDA (*interrupting*). We're going to have problems with that maid.

MISS TESMAN. With Berta? Problems?

TESMAN. What d'you mean, darling?

HEDDA (*pointing*). Look. Here on this chair. She's left her old hat.

TESMAN *drops the slippers in his agitation.*

TESMAN. Hedda . . .

HEDDA. Suppose someone came, and saw?

TESMAN. Hedda, that's aunt Julia's hat.

HEDDA. Really?

MISS TESMAN (*taking the hat*). Yes, Hedda, mine. And it's certainly not old.

HEDDA. I didn't look closely.

MISS TESMAN (*pinning on the hat*). As it happens, this is the first time I've worn it. The very first time.

TESMAN. It's a wonderful hat. Magnificent.

MISS TESMAN. Now, Jørgen, it's nothing of the kind.

She searches.

My parasol . . . ? Yes, here. (*Taking it.*) This is mine too. (*Tightly.*) Not Berta's.

TESMAN. New hat and parasol! Eh, Hedda?

HEDDA. Very nice.

TESMAN. Of course. Of course. Now, auntie, before you go, take a proper look at Hedda. Isn't she beautiful? Isn't she a picture?

MISS TESMAN. Well, of course she is. She's been special all her life.

She nods and crosses right. TESMAN *follows.*

TESMAN. But don't you think she looks well? Don't you think she's filled out on our travels, rounded out?

HEDDA (*crossing the room*). That's enough.

MISS TESMAN (*turning*). Rounded out?

TESMAN. Yes, auntie. You can't see it. That dress . . . But I can, I'm privileged –

HEDDA (*by the screen door; shortly*). Privileged!

TESMAN. It's the Alpine air, the mountain air.

HEDDA (*interrupting curtly*). I haven't changed since the day we left.

TESMAN. So you keep saying. But you have. You have. Hasn't she, auntie?

MISS TESMAN *has clasped her hands and is gazing at* HEDDA.

MISS TESMAN. Special. That's what Hedda is.

She goes to her, puts her hands round her head to bend it forwards, and kisses her hair.

God bless and protect Mrs Hedda Tesman. For Jørgen's sake.

HEDDA (*gently breaking free*). Do let go.

MISS TESMAN (*with quiet force*). I'll come every day to see you both.

TESMAN. Yes, auntie, please.

MISS TESMAN. Goodbye for now. Goodbye.

She goes out through the hall, accompanied by TESMAN. *They leave the door ajar, and* TESMAN *can be heard thanking her for the slippers and sending Aunt Rina his love. Meanwhile,* HEDDA *paces the room, arms folded, as if beside herself. She flings aside the curtains from the screen door and looks out. Almost at once,* TESMAN *returns, closing the door after him. He picks up his slippers, and starts wrapping them to put on the table.*

TESMAN. What are you looking at, Hedda?

HEDDA (*calm once again*). I was looking at the leaves. So yellow, so withered.

TESMAN. We are in September.

HEDDA (*edgy again*). So we are. So soon. September.

TESMAN. Aunt Julia was a little odd, didn't you think? Almost like a stranger. You've no idea why, have you?

HEDDA. I hardly know her. Isn't that what she's usually like?

TESMAN. Not like today.

HEDDA (*moving from the screen door*). D'you think that hat business offended her?

TESMAN. No. A little perhaps. At first. Just for a moment.

HEDDA. Such extraordinary behaviour, throwing it down in the sitting room like that. No one does that.

TESMAN. She won't do it again.

HEDDA. I'll sort things out with her.

TESMAN. Darling, if only you would.

HEDDA. When you go there this afternoon, invite her over this evening.

TESMAN. Of course I will. And Hedda, there's something you could do which would give her so much pleasure.

HEDDA. What?

TESMAN. Call her Auntie. For my sake. Hedda . . . ?

HEDDA. No, Tesman. I told you when you asked before. Miss Tesman she is, and Miss Tesman she stays.

TESMAN. It's just . . . now you're one of the family . . .

HEDDA (*moving upstage*). I wonder . . .

TESMAN (*following*). What is it, Hedda?

HEDDA. My old piano. It doesn't look right, in here.

TESMAN. When my first month's salary comes, we'll change it.

HEDDA. I don't want to change it. I don't want rid of it. We'll put it in the back room, and get another one in here. As soon as we can, I mean.

TESMAN (*subdued*). As soon as we can. Of course.

HEDDA (*picking up the flowers from the piano*). These flowers weren't here last night.

TESMAN. Aunt Julia must have brought them.

HEDDA (*looking inside the bouquet*). A visiting card. (*Reading.*) 'Will call later.' You'll never guess who it's from.

TESMAN. I can't imagine.

HEDDA. Mrs Elvsted. Look.

TESMAN. Mrs Elvsted! The solicitor's wife. She used to be Miss Rysing.

HEDDA. And she kept flaunting that confounded hair. An old flame of yours, they said.

TESMAN (*with a laugh*). Hedda, that was years ago. Before I met you. Fancy her coming into town.

HEDDA. And coming here. A social call. I remember her vaguely from high school.

TESMAN. I haven't seen her for – goodness knows how long. How can she stand it so far from town, in that poky little place?

HEDDA (*suddenly*). Tesman, wasn't it there, out of town, somewhere . . . ? Didn't Ejlert Løvborg –

TESMAN. He did! Out of town. That's right.

Enter BERTA *from the hall.*

BERTA. She's here again, madam, the lady who left the flowers. (*Pointing.*) Those flowers, madam.

HEDDA. Please show her in.

BERTA *opens the door to admit* MRS ELVSTED, *and then goes out.* MRS ELVSTED *is slim, with a soft, pretty face. Large blue eyes, slightly prominent; a nervous manner. Blonde, almost yellow hair, unusually luxuriant and curly. She is some two years younger than* HEDDA. *Her formal wear is dark and well cut, but not in the latest style. She is agitated, struggling for self-control.* HEDDA *goes to welcome her in a friendly way.*

HEDDA. Mrs Elvsted, good morning. How nice to meet you again.

MRS ELVSTED. It was a long time ago.

TESMAN (*shaking hands*). I remember you too.

HEDDA. Thank you for the flowers. Delightful.

MRS ELVSTED. I'd have come at once, yesterday afternoon. But they said you were away.

TESMAN. You've just arrived in town?

MRS ELVSTED. Yesterday lunchtime. When they told me you were away, I didn't know what to do.

HEDDA. How, what to do?

TESMAN. My dear Miss Rysing . . . Mrs Elvsted, I beg your pardon . . .

HEDDA. Is something wrong?

MRS ELVSTED. Yes. And I don't know anyone else. I've no one else to turn to.

HEDDA *puts the flowers down on the table.*

HEDDA. Sit on the sofa, here with me.

MRS ELVSTED. How can I sit? I haven't . . . I can't . . .

HEDDA. It's all right. Sit down.

She pulls MRS ELVSTED *to the sofa, and sits beside her.*

TESMAN. Now, dear lady, how can we help?

HEDDA. Is something wrong at home?

MRS ELVSTED. Yes. No. Both. I don't want you to misunderstand.

HEDDA. In that case, best say it, say it right out.

TESMAN. That's why you came.

MRS ELVSTED. That's why I came. In case . . . in case you don't know . . . Ejlert Løvborg's here in town.

HEDDA. Løvborg!

TESMAN. Ejlert Løvborg back. Amazing! Hedda –

HEDDA. I heard.

MRS ELVSTED. He's been here a week now. A whole week. Alone in this dreadful place. So many temptations.

HEDDA. But, dear Mrs Elvsted, why should you be so concerned?

MRS ELVSTED (*with a frightened glance at her*). He was the children's tutor.

HEDDA. Your children?

MRS ELVSTED. My husband's. I've none of my own.

HEDDA. Your stepchildren.

MRS ELVSTED. Yes.

TESMAN (*carefully*). Was he . . . how shall I put this? . . . was he *fit* for that?

MRS ELVSTED. No one's said a word against him these last two years.

TESMAN. Two years. Did you hear that, Hedda?

HEDDA. I heard.

MRS ELVSTED. Not a breath of scandal. Nothing. But now, when I know he's here, in the city, with money in his pockets, I'm afraid for him.

TESMAN. Why didn't he stay where he was? With you and your husband?

MRS ELVSTED. As soon as his book came out, he was so restless. So on edge. He couldn't stay with us.

TESMAN. That's right. Aunt Julia said he'd a new book out.

MRS ELVSTED. A big new book. *The Story of Civilisation*. Two weeks ago. And when it began to sell so well, and caused all that interest . . .

TESMAN. He wrote it some time ago . . . ? When he was . . . ?

MRS ELVSTED. Before, you mean.

TESMAN. Well, yes.

MRS ELVSTED. He wrote it while he was with us. All of it. In the last twelve months.

TESMAN. That's wonderful! Isn't that wonderful, Hedda?

MRS ELVSTED. If only it lasts.

HEDDA. Have you found him yet?

MRS ELVSTED. Not yet. It was hard getting hold of his address. But I found it at last, this morning.

HEDDA (*with a sharp look*). I'm surprised your husband –

MRS ELVSTED (*startled*). What d'you mean?

HEDDA. – should send you to town, on that kind of errand. Why didn't he come himself, or send one of his friends?

MRS ELVSTED. He hasn't time. In any case, I . . . I had some shopping.

HEDDA (*smiling*). Of course.

MRS ELVSTED (*jumping up nervously*). Mr Tesman, please, if Ejlert Løvborg comes here, be nice to him. He will come, he will. You were such good friends before. Both studying the same subject . . . the same approach . . .

TESMAN. In those days, yes.

MRS ELVSTED. So please . . . Mr Tesman, Mrs Tesman . . . please be kind to him. Oh Mr Tesman, will you promise?

TESMAN. Of course, my dear Mrs Rysing.

HEDDA. Elvsted.

TESMAN. I'll do everything I can. Everything.

MRS ELVSTED. You're so kind, so generous . . . (*Shaking his hand.*) Thank you, thank you. (*Timidly.*) My husband thinks so much of him.

HEDDA (*getting up*). Tesman, write him a note. If you leave it up to him, he may not come.

TESMAN. Good idea, Hedda. Good idea.

HEDDA. Do it now. Right now.

MRS ELVSTED (*begging*). Oh please.

TESMAN. This very minute. Have you his address, Mrs . . . Mrs Elvsted?

MRS ELVSTED. Yes.

She gives him a piece of paper from her bag.

There.

TESMAN. Wonderful. I'll go in there. (*Looking round.*) Slippers, slippers. Ah.

He picks up the package.

HEDDA. Write a friendly letter . . . long . . .

TESMAN. I certainly will.

MRS ELVSTED. But don't tell him I asked. Please don't.

TESMAN. Of course not. No question. Now . . .

Exit right, through the inner room.

HEDDA (*quietly, close to* MRS ELVSTED). There! Two birds with one stone.

MRS ELVSTED. What d'you mean?

HEDDA. Couldn't you see I wanted him to go?

MRS ELVSTED. To write the letter –

HEDDA. And so that we could talk, alone.

MRS ELVSTED (*bewildered*). About all this.

HEDDA. Yes.

MRS ELVSTED (*alarmed*). Mrs Tesman, there isn't any more. There isn't.

HEDDA. Of course there is. That's obvious. There's a lot more. Come and sit down. Let's make ourselves comfortable.

She propels MRS ELVSTED *to the chair beside the stove, and herself sits on one of the stools.*

MRS ELVSTED (*looking nervously at her watch*). I didn't mean to stay.

HEDDA. There's no rush. Is there? Tell me a little: how are things are at home?

MRS ELVSTED. That's just what I didn't want to talk about.

HEDDA. Not even to me? We were at school together.

MRS ELVSTED. You were in a higher class. You terrified me.

HEDDA. How, terrified?

MRS ELVSTED. When we met on the stairs, you pulled my hair.

HEDDA. I did?

MRS ELVSTED. You said, once, you'd burn it off.

HEDDA. Just talk.

MRS ELVSTED. I know that now. But in those days, I believed everything. And over the years, we've moved so far apart. Our friends, our social lives . . .

HEDDA. Well, now we can move back again. D'you remember, at school, we called each other by our Christian names?

MRS ELVSTED. We didn't.

HEDDA. I remember clearly. We'll be such friends again, just like before.

She moves the stool closer.

I mean it.

She kisses her cheek.

You must call me Hedda.

MRS ELVSTED *clasps* HEDDA's *hands and pats them.*

MRS ELVSTED. You're so kind, so friendly. I'm not used to it.

HEDDA. Well. I'll do the same: I'll call you . . . Thora.

MRS ELVSTED. My name's Thea.

HEDDA. Of course it is. Thea. (*With a tender look.*) Poor Thea. Not much kindness, not much companionship at home?

MRS ELVSTED. I don't have a home. I never have.

HEDDA (*after a short pause, gazing at her*). I thought that might be it.

MRS ELVSTED (*staring dully ahead*). Never.

HEDDA. I don't remember the details . . . When you first went out of town, to the solicitor's, wasn't it as housekeeper?

MRS ELVSTED. Governess. But his wife – his late wife – was an invalid . . . bedridden. I ran the house.

HEDDA. And you ended up . . . its mistress.

MRS ELVSTED (*dully*). That's right.

HEDDA. And now . . . how long is it now?

MRS ELVSTED. Since I married him?

HEDDA. Yes.

MRS ELVSTED. Five years.

HEDDA. Of course.

MRS ELVSTED. Five years! And the last two or three . . . Oh Mrs Tesman, if you only knew –

HEDDA (*lightly slapping her wrist*). Thea! Mrs Tesman . . . ?

MRS ELVSTED. I'm sorry. I will try. Oh . . . Hedda . . . if you only knew . . .

HEDDA (*offhand*). Wasn't it three years ago that Ejlert Løvborg moved out there?

MRS ELVSTED (*looking enquiringly at her*). Ejlert Løvborg? I suppose so.

HEDDA. Didn't you know him before? From the old days, here?

MRS ELVSTED. I knew his name, of course.

HEDDA. And when he moved out there . . . he visited you and your husband?

MRS ELVSTED. Every day. He gave the children lessons. By then, I couldn't manage everything myself.

HEDDA. Of course not. And your husband's . . . often away on business?

MRS ELVSTED. Mrs – Hedda – you understand. It's his work . . . he has to go . . .

HEDDA *leans on the arm of the chair.*

HEDDA. Poor little Thea, what is it? Tell me everything.

MRS ELVSTED. Ask what you want to know. I'll answer.

HEDDA. What sort of man is your husband, Thea? What's he like – at home, with you? Is he . . . kind to you?

MRS ELVSTED (*evasively*). He . . . thinks so.

HEDDA. He must be older than you. Much older. Twelve years, at least.

MRS ELVSTED (*breaking out*). That too. One thing and another. I can't bear him. We've nothing in common, nothing at all.

HEDDA. But doesn't he care for you? In his own way?

MRS ELVSTED. I don't know if he cares or not. I'm useful to him. And I don't cost much. I'm cheap.

HEDDA. Silly.

MRS ELVSTED (*shaking her head*). It'll never change. He'll never change. He cares for no one but himself. And the children, perhaps, a little.

HEDDA. And Ejlert Løvborg.

MRS ELVSTED (*staring*). Ejlert Løvborg! What d'you mean?

HEDDA. Oh Thea . . . when he sends you here to find him. (*With an almost imperceptible smile.*) You told Tesman so yourself.

MRS ELVSTED (*uncomfortably*). Oh. Yes, I did. (*All at once, low.*) I might as well tell you. Now, not later. It'll come out anyway.

HEDDA. Thea. Tell me what?

MRS ELVSTED. The truth. My husband knows nothing about this.

HEDDA. Really?

MRS ELVSTED. How could he? He was away on business. I couldn't stand it any longer, Hedda. I'd have been alone up there. Alone.

HEDDA. So you –

MRS ELVSTED. I packed my things . . . just the essentials. Secretly. And I . . . left.

HEDDA. Without a second thought?

MRS ELVSTED. I took the train, here to town.

HEDDA. Thea, how could you dare?

MRS ELVSTED *gets up and goes to the table.*

MRS ELVSTED. What else could I do? What else was left?

HEDDA. But what will he say, your husband, when you go back home?

MRS ELVSTED (*staring*). Back home – to him?

HEDDA. That's right.

MRS ELVSTED. I'm not going back.

HEDDA *goes to her.*

HEDDA. You mean you've left him? Forever?

MRS ELVSTED. What else could I do?

HEDDA. But to go like that. So . . . openly.

MRS ELVSTED. You can't hide such things.

HEDDA. But Thea, what will people say?

MRS ELVSTED. Good heavens, let them say what they like.

Sadly, heavily, she sits on the sofa.

What else could I do?

HEDDA (*after a short pause*). And what will you do now? What kind of job – ?

MRS ELVSTED. All I can say is, I have to live here, where Ejlert Løvborg lives. If I'm to live at all.

HEDDA *moves a chair from the table, sits beside her and strokes her hands.*

HEDDA. Thea, Thea, how did it start, this . . . friendship between you and Ejlert Løvborg?

MRS ELVSTED. It . . . happened. Little by little. It was as if I'd some kind of power over him.

HEDDA. Power?

MRS ELVSTED. He gave up his old ways. I didn't ask him. I didn't dare. But he could see I disapproved. So he . . . gave up.

HEDDA (*hiding involuntary scorn*). You 'saved' him, Thea. That's what you mean. Isn't that what it's called?

MRS ELVSTED. He called it that himself. At the end. But he, too . . . He made me a real person, Hedda. He taught me how to think. To understand . . . one thing . . . and then another.

HEDDA. He gave you lessons?

MRS ELVSTED. Not proper lessons. He talked to me. About anything, everything. Then came the special, wonderful day when I was able to help with his work. He let me help him.

HEDDA. And you did?

MRS ELVSTED. Oh yes. When he wrote, we worked at everything together. The two of us.

HEDDA. Comrades in arms.

MRS ELVSTED (*eagerly*). Oh Hedda, that's what he said. I ought to be so happy. But I'm not. I don't know how long it'll last.

HEDDA. Don't you trust him?

MRS ELVSTED (*dully*). There's a shadow between us. A woman's shadow.

HEDDA (*looking narrowly at her*). D'you know whose?

MRS ELVSTED. Some woman . . . from his past. He's never forgotten her.

HEDDA. He's talked about it?

MRS ELVSTED. Once. Nothing specific.

HEDDA. What did he say?

MRS ELVSTED. When they parted, he said, she wanted to shoot him with a pistol.

HEDDA (*icily calm*). Amazing. No one does that.

MRS ELVSTED. I thought it must be that singer, that redhaired creature he –

HEDDA. It must have been.

MRS ELVSTED. People said she always carried a loaded gun.

HEDDA. That proves it was her.

MRS ELVSTED (*wringing her hands*). Oh Hedda, they say she's . . . she's here. What can I do?

HEDDA (*glancing towards the inner room*). Shh! Tesman.

She gets up and whispers.

This is our secret, Thea.

MRS ELVSTED (*jumping up*). In God's name, yes.

Enter TESMAN *from the inner room right, with a letter in his hand.*

TESMAN. There. Written and ready.

HEDDA. Good. Now Mrs Elvsted really has to go. You stay here. I'll go to the gate with her.

TESMAN. Would you ask Berta to see to this?

HEDDA (*taking the letter*). I'll tell her.

Enter BERTA *from the hall.*

BERTA. Madam, His Honour Judge Brack is here.

HEDDA. Ask the gentleman in. Oh, and post this letter, will you?

BERTA (*taking the letter*). Yes, madam.

She holds the door for BRACK, *then goes out.* BRACK *is 45, stockily built but light in his movements. His face is round but fine-boned. Short, well-groomed hair, still mostly black. Bushy eyebrows; bright, sharp eyes. Full moustache, with shaped tips. He wears a fashionable morning suit, a little young for him. He uses an eyeglass, which he now and then lets fall. Hat in hand, he greets the company.*

BRACK. Not too early in the day?

HEDDA. Of course not.

TESMAN (*shaking hands*). You're welcome any time. (*Introducing them.*) Judge Brack, Miss Rysing . . .

HEDDA. Tst!

BRACK (*bowing*). Charmed.

HEDDA (*bantering*). How odd to see you in daylight for a change.

BRACK. Do I look so different?

HEDDA. A little younger.

BRACK. How kind.

TESMAN. And what d'you think of Hedda? Doesn't she look well? Doesn't she look –

HEDDA. Enough about me. Thank His Honour for all his hard work –

BRACK. Believe me, a pleasure.

HEDDA. Such a good friend. But here's my other friend standing, burning to be off. Excuse me, Your Honour. I won't be a moment.

A round of goodbyes, then she and MRS ELVSTED *go out through the hall.*

BRACK. Well. Is she pleased, your lady wife?

TESMAN. We can't thank you enough. A few changes here and there, I gather. One or two things still needed.

BRACK. Really?

TESMAN. But don't you trouble yourself. Hedda said she'd see to them herself. Do sit down. Sit down.

BRACK. Thank you.

He sits at the table.

My dear Tesman, there is one thing we ought to discuss.

TESMAN. Ah!

He sits.

The spectre at the feast? Go on.

BRACK. The money side's fine. Moving more slowly than I'd like, and a touch extravagant . . .

TESMAN. My dear man, this is for Hedda. I couldn't ask Hedda to live in one of those little suburban boxes.

BRACK. No, no, no.

TESMAN. In any case, it won't be long now, God willing, till I get my professorship.

BRACK. These things can take their time.

TESMAN. You've still heard nothing?

BRACK. Nothing certain. (*Sudden change of tone.*) There is one thing I have to tell you.

TESMAN. What?

BRACK. Your old friend Ejlert Løvborg's back. Here, in town.

TESMAN. She told us, the lady who went out with Hedda.

BRACK. What was her name? I didn't quite catch it.

TESMAN. Mrs Elvsted.

BRACK. Of course. Her husband's a solicitor. Løvborg's been out there, staying with them.

TESMAN. And have you heard? Wonderful news! He's back on the rails again.

BRACK. So people say.

TESMAN. He's even published a book.

BRACK. That's right.

TESMAN. And made quite a stir.

BRACK. I believe so.

TESMAN. Well that's wonderful! So talented . . . I was afraid he'd gone astray for good.

BRACK. Everyone thought so.

TESMAN. But what on Earth will he do now? What on Earth will he live on?

During this, HEDDA *comes back through the hall.*

HEDDA (*to* BRACK). He's always the same. Always wondering what people are going to live on.

TESMAN. Oh Hedda. We were talking about that poor man Ejlert Løvborg.

HEDDA *gives him a sharp look.*

HEDDA. Really. (*Lightly.*) Why d'you call him poor?

TESMAN. He must have run through his inheritance years ago. And he can't produce a new book every year. So I was wondering, what's he going to do?

BRACK. I may have news about that.

TESMAN. Really?

BRACK. He's well-connected. Influential relatives.

TESMAN. Relatives who want nothing to do with him, unfortunately.

BRACK. They used to call him their golden boy.

TESMAN. Until he spoiled it, spoiled everything.

HEDDA. One never knows. (*With a light laugh.*) After all, they 'saved' him at the Elvsteds'.

BRACK. And there is this book of his.

TESMAN. Let's hope it leads him somewhere. I've just sent him a letter. Hedda, I invited him here this evening.

BRACK. Oh Tesman. My dinner-party tonight. Bachelors and husbands only. You promised yesterday, on the pier.

HEDDA. Tesman, you'd forgotten.

TESMAN. So I had.

BRACK. Well, it doesn't matter. He won't turn up.

TESMAN. Why ever not?

With some reluctance, BRACK *gets up and stands with his hands on the chair-back.*

BRACK. Tesman . . . Mrs Tesman . . . I think you really should be told. It's something –

TESMAN. To do with Ejlert Løvborg?

BRACK. With him and with you.

TESMAN. My dear Brack, what is it?

BRACK. Your professorship . . . may not come through as quickly as you'd like, as you'd expect . . .

TESMAN *(jumping up in alarm)*. There's a problem. What is it?

BRACK. There may be . . . competition.

TESMAN. Competition! Did you hear that, Hedda?

HEDDA *(leaning back in the chair)*. I heard.

TESMAN. But who with? Surely not with –

BRACK. Exactly. Ejlert Løvborg.

TESMAN *(clasping his hands)*. I don't believe it. It's impossible.

BRACK. It may still happen.

TESMAN. But Brack, this is hardly fair. To me.

He gestures.

I'm a married man. Hedda and I . . . We married because of my prospects. We plunged into debt, even borrowed from Aunt Julia. I was as good as promised that professorship.

BRACK. Now, now. It's yours, no question. But first there'll be a competition.

HEDDA (*at ease in the chair*). Ha, Tesman, it's like a tournament.

TESMAN. Hedda, darling, how can you make a joke of it?

HEDDA (*as before*). I'm hanging on the outcome.

BRACK. Whatever the outcome, Mrs Tesman, I thought you ought to know. The way things are. Especially since I hear you're planning . . . purchases.

HEDDA. This makes no difference.

BRACK. In that case . . . please excuse me. (*To* TESMAN.) When I go for my constitutional this afternoon, I'll call for you.

TESMAN. I . . . I don't know what to . . .

HEDDA (*lying back, stretching out her hand*). Goodbye, Your Honour. Come again soon.

BRACK. Thank you. Goodbye. Goodbye.

TESMAN (*accompanying him to the door*). Goodbye, old man. I do apologise . . .

Exit BRACK *through the hall.* TESMAN *paces.*

TESMAN. Oh Hedda, people should never live in fairy tales.

HEDDA (*looking at him and smiling*). Is that what you do?

TESMAN. That's what we did. Getting married, setting up house on nothing but my prospects . . . a fairy tale.

HEDDA. If you say so.

TESMAN. Well, at least we have our home. Our beautiful home. The home we dreamed of, swooned over, almost. Both of us.

HEDDA (*getting up slowly, heavily*). We agreed on a certain style . . . a certain standard of living.

TESMAN. Of course we did. And I really looked forward to it: seeing you at the heart of things, in a house of your own, with a throng of guests. Wonderful! It's just that . . . for the moment, it'll have to be just the two of us, Hedda. We can invite Aunt Julia now and then. Oh, this was never for you. Things should have been so different.

HEDDA. No footman, yet.

TESMAN. I'm afraid not. Out of the question.

HEDDA. And the horse I hoped for? –

TESMAN (*startled*). Horse?

HEDDA. I mustn't even think about riding now.

TESMAN. Good heavens, no.

HEDDA (*crossing the room*). Thank goodness I've one thing left. I can still amuse myself.

TESMAN (*overjoyed*). Wonderful. What is it, Hedda? What is it you have?

From the rear door, HEDDA *looks at him with scorn.*

HEDDA. My pistols . . . Jørgen.

TESMAN (*horrified*). Pistols!

HEDDA (*cold-eyed*). General Gabler's pistols.

Exit. TESMAN *runs to the door and shouts after her.*

TESMAN. No, Hedda! For God's sake! They're dangerous. Please, Hedda! I beg you. No!

ACT TWO

The scene is the same as in Act One, except that the piano has been replaced by an elegant little writing-desk and bookcase. A side-table stands beside the sofa left. Most of the flowers have gone, though MRS ELVSTED'*s bouquet is on the large table centre stage. It is afternoon.* HEDDA *is alone in the room. She wears afternoon dress. She stands by the open screen door, loading a pistol. The gun's twin is in an open pistol-case on the writing-desk.*

HEDDA (*calling into the garden*). Your Honour. Hello again.

BRACK (*in the distance, off*). Mrs Tesman, hello.

   HEDDA *lifts the pistol and takes aim.*

HEDDA. Your Honour, I'm going to shoot you.

BRACK (*shouting from below*). Don't point that thing at me.

HEDDA. If you will use the back way in.

   She fires.

BRACK (*nearer*). Are you out of your mind?

HEDDA. I didn't hit you. Did I?

BRACK (*still outside*). Don't play the fool.

HEDDA. Come in, Your Honour. Come in.

   BRACK *comes in by the screen door. He is dressed for his party, with a light coat over his arm.*

BRACK. What on Earth are you doing? This isn't the first time. What are you shooting at?

HEDDA. The sky. I stand and shoot the sky.

BRACK *takes the pistol gently.*

BRACK. Excuse me . . . (*Examining it.*) I remember this one. (*Looking round.*) Where's the case? Ah, here.

He puts the pistol in its case and shuts it.

No more games today.

HEDDA. What else am I to do, in Heaven's name?

BRACK. Has no one called?

HEDDA (*closing the screen door*). Not a soul. Everyone we know must still be in the country.

BRACK. Isn't Tesman back yet?

HEDDA (*putting the pistol-case in the drawer of the writing-desk*). No. Straight after lunch, off he ran to his aunties. He wasn't expecting you so soon.

BRACK. I should have thought of that. Silly of me.

HEDDA (*turning and looking at him*). Silly?

BRACK. If I had thought, I'd have come – even earlier.

HEDDA (*crossing the room*). There'd have been no one at home at all. I was in my room, changing after lunch.

BRACK. And no cracks in the door, for making conversation.

HEDDA. One arrangement you forgot.

BRACK. Silly again.

HEDDA. We'd better sit down here, and wait. Tesman won't be long. He'll be home any minute.

BRACK. I'll possess my soul in patience.

HEDDA sits at one end of the sofa. BRACK *lays his coat over the back of the nearest chair and sits down, still holding his hat. Short pause. They look at each other.*

HEDDA. Well now.

BRACK (*same tone*). Well now.

HEDDA. I said it first.

BRACK (*leaning forward*). Let's make polite conversation, Mrs Tesman.

HEDDA (*leaning back in the sofa*). It does seem an age since you and I last talked. A few pleasantries last night, this morning – I don't count those.

BRACK. The two of us. Alone, you mean?

HEDDA. Something like that.

BRACK. I called every single day, praying you were home from your travels.

HEDDA. I prayed the same thing, every single day.

BRACK. Dear Mrs Tesman, I thought you were having such a wonderful time.

HEDDA. You can't imagine.

BRACK. That's what Tesman wrote.

HEDDA. Oh, he did. Rooting about in libraries. Copying ancient manuscripts. Wonderful!

BRACK (*with a touch of malice*). It's what he was put in the world to do. Most of the time.

HEDDA. Exactly. Always busy. But I wasn't, Brack! I was bored. So . . . bored.

BRACK (*sympathetically*). You're serious. You really mean it.

HEDDA. Of course I mean it. Six months without meeting anyone from . . . from our circle. Shared interests. Someone to talk to.

BRACK. I know what you mean.

HEDDA. And hardest of all –

BRACK. What?

HEDDA. To be with the same individual, every second, day after day after day –

BRACK (*nodding agreement*). Day and night . . .

HEDDA. I said: every second.

BRACK. But Tesman, dear Tesman . . . Surely . . .

HEDDA. For Heaven's sake! He's a . . . a scholar.

BRACK. True.

HEDDA. And scholars are not good company on journeys. Not day after day after day.

BRACK. Not even . . . scholars one loves?

HEDDA. Don't be silly.

BRACK (*surprised*). Pardon, Hedda?

HEDDA (*half joking, half cross*). You should try it. The history of civilisation, day and night.

BRACK. Every second.

HEDDA. Domestic crafts in the fourteenth century. What could be worse?

BRACK (*looking narrowly at her*). Are you saying . . . ? D'you really mean . . . ?

HEDDA. That Tesman and I can't make a match of it?

BRACK. If you like.

HEDDA. Good lord, does it surprise you?

BRACK. Yes. And no.

HEDDA. I'd danced myself out. That was all. My time was up. (*Checking herself.*) No, I mustn't say that. Not even think it.

BRACK. You've really no cause –

HEDDA. Oh, cause. (*Looking carefully at him.*) In any case, Jørgen Tesman . . . such a model husband.

BRACK. And such a good soul. No doubt of it.

HEDDA. I don't think he's a fool. Do you?

BRACK. Not exactly –

HEDDA. So . . . tireless. Bound to get there in the end.

BRACK (*looking at her quizzically*). I assumed you were like everyone else: thought he was on his way.

HEDDA (*wearily*). Yes. I did. And he was so determined . . . so sure he'd be able to support me . . . Why should I turn him down?

BRACK. What other choice had you?

HEDDA. Your Honour, I don't remember any of my other admirers making a similar offer.

BRACK (*with a laugh*). I can't answer for all the others, Mrs Tesman. But me: you know what enormous respect I've always had for . . . the marriage tie. In theory.

HEDDA (*mocking*). Oh, I never had hopes of you.

BRACK. All I ask of life is a circle of close friends . . . people I can help and advise, places I can come and go as I please, as a trusted friend of –

HEDDA. – the husband.

BRACK (*leaning forward*). Well, frankly, I'd prefer the wife. But the husband will do. I tell you, this kind of . . . triangular relationship . . . can be highly satisfying for all three parties.

HEDDA. I often longed for a third party on that trip. To sit in a carriage side by side with just one man –

BRACK. But the honeymoon journey's over now.

HEDDA (*shaking her head*). There's still the marriage journey. On and on. This is just a temporary stop.

BRACK. Exactly. One jumps out . . . one stretches one's legs . . .

HEDDA. I won't jump out.

BRACK. You won't?

HEDDA. Some of us –

BRACK (*laughing*). Watch our step.

HEDDA. Exactly.

BRACK. You're joking.

HEDDA (*gesturing 'No'*). I don't want that. I prefer to stay where I am. Sitting side by side.

BRACK. But suppose a third person did join the party?

HEDDA. That's different.

BRACK. A trusted friend. A soul-mate.

HEDDA. Making interesting conversation about all kinds of things.

BRACK. And a total stranger to scholarship.

HEDDA (*sighing audibly*). A change indeed.

The hall door is heard opening and closing.

BRACK. The triangle is complete.

HEDDA (*low*). And the train goes on.

Enter TESMAN *from the hall. He is wearing a grey outdoor suit and a trilby. He is carrying an armful of journals and magazines, and his pockets are stuffed with more of them. He goes to put them down on the table by the corner sofa.*

TESMAN. Phew. Far too hot to be carting all these around.

He puts them down.

Look, Hedda, I'm sweating like a pig. Ah, Brack, you're here. Why didn't Berta say?

BRACK *(getting up)*. I came through the garden.

HEDDA. Magazines. What are they?

TESMAN *(turning them over)*. Not magazines, journals. Learned journals. New issues I had to have.

HEDDA. Learned journals.

BRACK. Learned journals, Mrs Tesman.

They smile pointedly at one another.

HEDDA. You need more learned journals?

TESMAN. It's not a case of more. One has to have them all. One has to keep up.

HEDDA. Ah. So one does.

TESMAN *(rooting in the pile)*. I managed to get Ejlert Løvborg's new book too.

He finds it.

You'd like a look at that, Hedda. Wouldn't you?

HEDDA. No thanks. Yes. Some other time.

TESMAN. I dipped into it on the way.

BRACK. And how does it seem to you . . . a colleague?

TESMAN. Remarkable. Rational. Objective. It's like nothing else he's ever written.

He gathers the magazines.

I'll take these in. I can't wait to cut the pages! And I really must change. (*To* BRACK.) We're not rushing off this minute, are we?

BRACK. Take as long as you like.

TESMAN. As long as I like. Right. (*With the magazines, at the door.*) Oh, Hedda, Aunt Julia won't be coming this evening.

HEDDA. Not that business with the hat . . . ?

TESMAN. How can you think such a thing? Aunt Julia? No no. Aunt Rina's poorly.

HEDDA. She always is.

TESMAN. Poor soul, she's really bad today.

HEDDA. Then of course the other one must stay. I understand.

TESMAN. She was so delighted, Aunt Julia, to see how you've put on weight while we were away.

HEDDA (*to herself, getting up*). Never-ending aunts!

TESMAN. Pardon?

HEDDA (*crossing to the screen door*). Nothing.

TESMAN. Well . . . excuse me . . .

Exit right through the inner room.

BRACK. What business with the hat?

HEDDA. Just something with Miss Tesman this morning. She left her hat on a chair. (*Grinning at him.*) I pretended I thought it was Berta's.

BRACK (*shaking his head*). Mrs Tesman, how could you? Such a sweet old lady . . . !

HEDDA (*edgy, crossing the room*). I . . . it's . . .

She sits heavily in the chair by the stove.

Sometimes I just have to. I can't explain.

BRACK (*behind the chair*). You're unhappy. That's all it is.

HEDDA (*gazing into the distance*). And tell me. Why should I be . . . happy?

BRACK. Among other things . . . you've got the house you longed for.

HEDDA (*mocking him*). Just like a fairy tale. You believe that?

BRACK. Not true?

HEDDA. Not entirely.

BRACK. Ha!

HEDDA. This is what's true. Last summer I used Tesman to escort me home after evening parties.

BRACK. Unfortunately I went a different way.

HEDDA. Yes. You went a different way last summer.

BRACK (*laughing*). Mrs Tesman! Go on. You and Tesman . . .

HEDDA. One evening we came this way. Tesman was . . . wriggling and writhing. He'd run out of conversation. I took pity on him –

BRACK (*smiling in disbelief*). Really?

HEDDA. To help him out, I said, just for something to say, that I wouldn't mind living here one day.

BRACK. Nothing else?

HEDDA. Not then.

BRACK. But later?

HEDDA. I should have known. One should think before one speaks.

BRACK. One never does.

HEDDA. Thanks. It was passion for this villa, the widow
Falk's villa, that brought us together. Tesman and me.
Engagement, marriage, honeymoon – all of it. I should
have known. I nearly said: As you make your bed, so you're
bound to lie on it.

BRACK. So you didn't really like the house?

HEDDA. Not at all.

BRACK. But now? Now we've made it . . . cosy for you.

HEDDA. I can smell nothing but lavender, dried roses, in
every room. I blame Aunt Julia.

BRACK (*laughing*). More likely the late widow Falk.

HEDDA. 'Late' is right. Or the flowers from yesterday's ball.

*She clasps her hands behind her head, leans back in the chair and
looks at him.*

Dear Brack, you can't imagine how bored I'm going to be
here.

BRACK. Oh surely, Mrs Tesman, life will find something to
offer you.

HEDDA. Something . . . absorbing?

BRACK. If you're lucky.

HEDDA. What will it be? What could it be? I sometimes
wonder . . . (*Interrupting herself.*) Out of the question.

BRACK. What is?

HEDDA. Just: I wonder if I could persuade Tesman to go into
politics.

BRACK (*laughing*). You're joking. Tesman! Politics! Not his style
at all.

HEDDA. All the same, if I could persuade him . . .

BRACK. But why should you want to? If he's not cut out for it . . . Why should you want to?

HEDDA. I told you. Because I'm bored.

Short pause.

You really think it's out of the question? Tesman . . . in parliament?

BRACK. You don't understand. If he'd been rich to start with . . .

HEDDA (*jumping up*). Genteel poverty! Again! I married it!

She paces.

It makes everything mean, ridiculous. It does. It does.

BRACK. I think there's something else.

HEDDA. What?

BRACK. In your whole life, you've never had anything really . . . serious to think about.

HEDDA. What d'you mean?

BRACK. But now, things may change.

HEDDA (*tossing her head*). You mean this wretched professorship. That's Tesman's affair. Entirely. I won't waste my brain on that.

BRACK. Hmhm. I didn't mean that. I meant . . . how can I put it . . . something vital . . . vitally dependent. On you. (*Smiling.*) Dependent on you, Mrs Tesman.

HEDDA (*furious*). No! Don't even think such things.

BRACK (*carefully*). We'll see. In a very few months. We'll see.

HEDDA (*curtly*). I've no talent for that, Your Honour. No talent for . . . things that depend on me.

BRACK. You're a woman. It's a woman's . . . talent. Her calling.

HEDDA (*at the screen door*). I said: no! I've only one talent. I decided that long ago.

BRACK (*going towards her*). For what? If you don't mind me asking.

HEDDA (*standing there, looking out*). For boring myself to death.

She turns, glances into the inner room and laughs.

Ah! Here he comes . . . the professor.

BRACK (*quietly, warning*). Mrs Tesman . . .

Enter TESMAN, *from the inner room right. He is dressed for the dinner-party, and carries his hat and gloves.*

TESMAN. Hedda, we've not had Eilert's answer yet? That he isn't coming?

HEDDA. No.

TESMAN. He'll be here any minute then. You'll see.

BRACK. You really think he'll come?

TESMAN. I'm sure he will. Almost. That was all just gossip, what you told us this morning.

BRACK. Ah.

TESMAN. Aunt Julia said she was certain he wouldn't stand in my way again. Certain.

BRACK. That's fine, then.

TESMAN puts his hat and gloves down on a chair, right.

TESMAN. I really ought to wait for him, as long as possible.

BRACK. We've time. There'll be no one there till seven . . . half past . . .

TESMAN. We can keep Hedda company till then. Pass the time.

HEDDA *lays* BRACK's *coat and hat on the corner sofa.*

HEDDA. If all else fails, Mr Løvborg can stay here with me.

BRACK (*trying to take his coat and hat*). Dear lady! What d'you mean, if all else fails?

HEDDA. If he doesn't want to go with you and Tesman.

TESMAN (*looking at her doubtfully*). Hedda, darling . . . D'you think it's all right, for him to be here with you? I mean, Aunt Julia can't come.

HEDDA. Mrs Elvsted's coming. We'll take tea together. The three of us.

TESMAN. Of course!

BRACK (*with a smile*). In any case, that might be best for him.

HEDDA. What d'you mean?

BRACK. Good gracious, dear lady, haven't you heard about my dinner-parties? They're only for men of iron self-discipline.

HEDDA. But that's what Mr Løvborg is these days. One sinner who repented . . .

Enter BERTA *from the hall.*

BERTA. Madam, there's a gentleman –

HEDDA. Show him in.

TESMAN (*quietly*). It's him. I knew!

Enter LØVBORG *from the hall. He is the same age as* TESMAN, *but looks older and worse preserved. He is slight and gaunt. Dark brown hair and beard. Long, pale face, with patches of colour on the cheekbones. Stylish, almost new, afternoon clothes, dark gloves, a stovepipe hat. He stops by the door and bows awkwardly, seemingly embarrassed.* TESMAN *goes and shakes his hand.*

TESMAN. My dear Ejlert. How good to see you again.

LØVBORG (*in a low voice*). Jørgen, thanks for your note.

He goes to HEDDA.

Mrs Tesman.

HEDDA (*shaking his hand*). Mr Løvborg. (*Gesturing.*) Do you two gentlemen . . . ?

LØVBORG (*bowing slightly*). Judge Brack, isn't it?

BRACK (*the same*). Of course we know each other. A year ago, I think.

TESMAN (*putting his hands on* LØVBORG's *shoulders*). My dear Ejlert, from now on you must treat this house as your own. Isn't that right, Hedda? You are coming back to town?

LØVBORG. That's right.

TESMAN. Wonderful! D'you know, I've just bought your book. Mind, I haven't had time to read it yet.

LØVBORG. I shouldn't bother.

TESMAN. Why ever not?

LØVBORG. It's a potboiler.

TESMAN. What d'you mean?

BRACK. Everyone admires it.

LØVBORG. I meant them to admire it. There isn't a word to disagree with.

BRACK. Sensible.

TESMAN. But Ejlert –

LØVBORG. I have to build my reputation up again. That's the whole point. From scratch.

TESMAN (*slightly embarrassed*). Yes. That's right.

LØVBORG smiles, puts down his hat and takes a large brown envelope from his pocket.

LØVBORG. But when this comes out, Jørgen, you'd better read it. A real piece of work. The real me.

TESMAN. What's it about?

LØVBORG. It's a continuation.

TESMAN. What of?

LØBORG. The book.

TESMAN. The new one?

LØVBORG. Exactly.

TESMAN. But Ejlert, that comes right to the present day.

LØVBORG. This is about the future.

TESMAN. The future? We've no information.

LØVBORG. But we can speculate.

He opens the envelope.

Look –

TESMAN. This isn't your writing.

LØVBORG. Dictated.

He turns the pages.

Two sections. Part One: Cultural Determinants in the Future. Part Two . . .

He finds it.

. . . Cultural Directions in the Future.

TESMAN. Amazing! I'd never have imagined such a subject.

HEDDA *is drumming her fingers on the screen door.*

HEDDA. Never.

LØVBORG *slides the manuscript back in the envelope, and puts it on the table.*

LØVBORG. I brought it with me because . . . I thought I might read you some this evening.

TESMAN. Very kind. But . . . this evening?

He glances at BRACK.

I don't see how . . .

LØVBORG. It's all right. Some other time. No hurry.

BRACK. The thing is, Mr Løvborg, I'm giving a dinner-party this evening. In Tesman's honour, as it happens . . .

LØVBORG (*reaching for his hat*). In that case . . .

BRACK. Look here, why don't you come too?

LØVBORG (*short and sharp*). No. Thank you, no.

BRACK. No, come. Just a few close friends. We'll be really quite 'jolly', as Hed – Mrs Tesman – puts it.

LØVBORG. I'm sure. But all the same I –

BRACK. You could bring your manuscript and read it to Tesman there. I've plenty of rooms.

TESMAN. Ejlert. It's not a bad idea . . .

HEDDA (*breaking in*). My dear man, if Mr Løvborg really doesn't want to . . . I'm sure he'd rather dine here, with me.

LØVBORG (*staring*). With you?

HEDDA. And Mrs Elvsted.

LØVBORG. Ah. (*Offhand.*) I ran into her this morning.

HEDDA. She'll be here tonight. So it's essential that you come. Otherwise, who'll see her safely home?

LØVBORG. That's true. Yes. Thank you, Mrs Tesman. I'll be glad to come.

HEDDA. I'll tell Berta.

She goes to the hall door and rings. BERTA comes in, and HEDDA talks quietly to her, pointing to the inner room. BERTA nods and exit.

TESMAN (*meanwhile, to* LØVBORG). Listen, Ejlert, this new stuff . . . the future . . . is that what your lectures are to be about?

LØVBORG. Yes.

TESMAN. They said in the bookshop that you're giving a course this autumn.

LØVBORG. Yes. I'm sorry, Jørgen.

TESMAN. No, no, no. I . . .

LØVBORG. I can see how annoying it must be for you.

TESMAN (*weakly*). Oh, I couldn't expect you to . . . for my sake . . .

LØVBORG. I am waiting till you've got your professorship.

TESMAN. Waiting! But you . . . You're not competing?

LØVBORG. You take the professorship; I'll take fame.

TESMAN. So Aunt Julia was right! I knew it. Hedda, Ejlert won't stand in our way at all.

HEDDA (*curtly*). Our way? Leave me out of it.

She goes to the inner room, where BERTA *is setting glassware on the table.* HEDDA *nods approvingly and comes in again. Exit* BERTA.

TESMAN (*meanwhile*). Brack, you heard this. What do you think?

BRACK. Reputation . . . fame . . . they're very attractive . . .

TESMAN. Attractive. But not . . . not . . .

HEDDA (*smiling icily at him*). You look as if you've been struck by lightning.

TESMAN. I . . . something like that . . .

BRACK. There were thunderclouds, Mrs Tesman. But they've passed, they've passed.

HEDDA (*gesturing towards the inner room*). Would you gentlemen care for a glass of cold punch?

BRACK (*looking at his watch*). A stirrup-cup? Not a bad idea.

TESMAN. Wonderful, Hedda. Wonderful. I feel so relieved, such a burden's been –

HEDDA. Mr Løvborg?

LØVBORG (*gesturing 'No'*). Not for me, thanks.

BRACK. For Heaven's sake, man. Cold punch is hardly poison.

LØVBORG. Not for everyone, perhaps.

HEDDA (*to* BRACK *and* TESMAN). You go in. I'll keep Mr Løvborg company.

TESMAN. Wonderful, Hedda. Yes.

During what follows, he and BRACK *go into the inner room, sit down, drink punch, smoke and talk animatedly.* HEDDA *goes to the writing-desk.* LØVBORG *stays by the stove.*

HEDDA (*loudly*). If you like, I'll show you some photographs. Tesman and I have just come back . . . from the Tyrol . . . our honeymoon . . .

She takes an album and puts it on the table by the sofa. She sits at one end of the sofa. LØVBORG approaches and stands looking down at her. Then he takes a chair and sits to her left with his back to the inner room.

HEDDA (*opening the album*). D'you see this range of mountains, Mr Løvborg? The Ortler Range. Tesman's written it underneath, look: 'The Ortler Range, from Melan'.

LØVBORG *has been gazing intently at her.*

LØVBORG (*softly and slowly*). Miss . . . Hedda . . . Gabler.

HEDDA (*glancing at him*). Tss!

LØVBORG (*as before*). Miss . . . Hedda . . . Gabler.

HEDDA (*looking through the album*). I was, once. When we knew each other . . . then.

LØVBORG. And never again? Must I make a resolution, never to utter those words again? Miss Hedda Gabler.

HEDDA (*turning the pages*). Make a resolution. Make it now.

LØVBORG (*in an injured tone*). Hedda Gabler, married? And to . . . Jørgen Tesman.

HEDDA. Exactly.

LØVBORG. Oh Hedda, how could you throw yourself away?

HEDDA (*with a sharp glance*). Shh!

LØVBORG. Why?

TESMAN *comes in and goes to the sofa.*

HEDDA (*in a bored voice*). Look, Mr Løvborg. This is the view from Ampezzo. Look at those mountains. (*With an affectionate glance up at* TESMAN.) What do they call these wonderful mountains, Tesman?

TESMAN. Which mountains? Oh, the Dolomites.

HEDDA. Of course. Mr Løvborg, the Dolomites.

TESMAN. Hedda, can't we bring in some punch? At least for you?

HEDDA. Yes please. And some biscuits, perhaps.

TESMAN. Cigarettes?

HEDDA. No.

TESMAN. All right.

He goes into the inner room, and exit right. BRACK *stays in the inner room, looking occasionally at* HEDDA *and* LØVBORG.

LØVBORG (*in a low voice, as before*). Hedda, darling, answer me. How could you . . . do this?

HEDDA (*apparently absorbed in the album*). If you keep calling me darling, I won't talk to you.

LØVBORG. When no one else is there?

HEDDA. You can think it. But you mustn't say it.

LØVBORG. It offends your love . . . for Tesman.

HEDDA (*with a quizzical smile at him*). Love?

LØVBORG. No love!

HEDDA. No . . . disloyalty. I won't have that.

LØVBORG. Hedda, tell me one thing –

HEDDA. Shh!

TESMAN *comes from the inner room with a tray.*

TESMAN. Time to enjoy yourselves!

He puts the tray on the table, and begins filling glasses.

HEDDA. Why did you fetch it?

TESMAN. My dear, I wait on you hand and foot.

HEDDA. You've filled both glasses. You know Mr Løvborg doesn't –

TESMAN. But Mrs Elvsted'll be here any minute.

HEDDA. Mrs Elvsted. Yes.

TESMAN. Had you forgotten?

HEDDA. We were so engrossed. (*Showing him a photo.*) D'you remember this village?

TESMAN. The one at the foot of the Brenner Pass. Where we spent the night –

HEDDA. And met all those jolly tourists.

TESMAN. That's right. You should've been with us, Ejlert! Ha ha!

He goes in again and sits with BRACK.

LØVBORG. Answer me one thing, Hedda.

HEDDA. What?

LØVBORG. Did you feel no love for me? A flicker . . . a spark . . . for me?

HEDDA. It's hard to say. I thought we were close. Close friends. Comrades in arms: no secrets. (*With a smile.*) You always said what was on your mind.

LØVBORG. You didn't mind.

HEDDA. When I think about it now . . . It was beautiful . . . exciting . . . daring. Secrets . . . We were comrades in arms. It was our secret, shared by no other living soul.

LØVBORG. Our secret. I called on your father every afternoon. He sat by the window, the General, reading the paper. His back to us –

HEDDA. We sat on the corner seat –

LØVBORG. Always looking at the same magazine –

HEDDA. Like this album, now.

LØVBORG. And Hedda, the things I told you! Things about myself. No one else knew, then. My drinking . . . days and nights on end. I sat there and told you. Days and nights. Oh Hedda, what gave you such power? To make me tell you . . . things like that?

HEDDA. You think I had power?

LØVBORG. What else would've made me tell you? All those questions . . . things you asked . . . indirectly . . .

HEDDA. You understood.

LØVBORG. The things you asked. Absolute trust.

HEDDA. Asked indirectly.

LØVBORG. Absolute trust. You asked – everything.

HEDDA. And you, Mr Løvborg, answered.

LØVBORG. Looking back, that's what I don't understand. Hedda, are you sure there wasn't love, deep down? When I confessed, didn't you want to absolve me, to wash away my sin?

HEDDA. Not exactly.

LØVBORG. What, then?

HEDDA. You really don't know? A young girl . . . without anyone knowing . . . her chance . . .

LØVBORG. Chance?

HEDDA. To glimpse a world that . . .

LØVBORG. That – ?

HEDDA. That she'd no business to know existed.

LØVBORG. That's all it was?

HEDDA. That's all it was. To me.

LØVBORG. We both longed to discover life. Comrades in arms. But why did it have to stop?

HEDDA. Your fault.

LØVBORG. You stopped it.

HEDDA. Before we grew . . . too close. How could you, Mr Løvborg? Absolute trust. Comrades in arms.

LØVBORG (*clenching his fists*). Oh, why didn't you do as you promised? You said you'd shoot me. Why didn't you?

HEDDA. Simple: the scandal.

LØVBORG. Well, well! Underneath, you're a coward.

HEDDA. Absolutely. (*New tone.*) Lucky for you, though. And you consoled yourself. Look what a time you've been having, at the Elvsteds'.

LØVBORG. I know what Thea's told you.

HEDDA. And have you told her – about us?

LØVBORG. Not a word. She wouldn't understand. She's a fool.

HEDDA. A fool?

LØVBORG. In things like that.

HEDDA. And I'm a coward.

She leans towards him, looks into his eyes, and says gently:

Now I'll confess to you.

LØVBORG (*tense*). What?

HEDDA. When I . . . didn't shoot you –

LØVBORG. Well?

HEDDA. That wasn't my worst cowardice, that evening.

LØVBORG *looks at her a moment, understands, and whispers passionately:*

LØVBORG. Hedda, darling. I see now. Comrades in arms. That was it. You and I. Your longing for life . . .

HEDDA (*in a low voice, and with an angry look*). That's enough. Enough.

It is getting dark. BERTA *opens the hall door.* HEDDA *snaps the album shut and calls out with a smile:*

Thea! So there you are. Come in.

MRS ELVSTED *comes in from the hall. She is wearing formal evening clothes. The door closes behind her.* HEDDA, *on the sofa, holds out her arms.*

You can't believe how glad I am to see you.

MRS ELVSTED, *who has gone to greet the men in the inner room, now comes back to the table, to shake* HEDDA's *hand.* LØVBORG *has stood up. He and* MRS ELVSTED *nod to each other, without speaking.*

MRS ELVSTED. I ought to go in and talk to your husband.

HEDDA. No. Leave them. They're just going out.

MRS ELVSTED. Going out?

HEDDA. Out on the town.

MRS ELVSTED (*quickly, to* LØVBORG). Not you as well?

LØVBORG. No.

HEDDA. Mr Løvborg's staying here with us.

> MRS ELVSTED *takes a chair and starts towards* LØVBORG *to sit by him.*

MRS ELVSTED. This is cosy. Cosy.

HEDDA. Not there, Thea. Darling. Over here, by me. I intend to come between you.

MRS ELVSTED. If that's what you want.

> *She goes round the table and sits on the sofa beside* HEDDA. LØVBORG *sits down again.*

LØVBORG (*after a short pause, to* HEDDA). Isn't she wonderful? To sit and look at?

HEDDA (*stroking* MRS ELVSTED*'s hair*). To look at?

LØVBORG. She and I . . . we really are comrades in arms. We sit together, absolute trust, we tell each other everything –

HEDDA. Not indirectly, Mr Løvborg?

LØVBORG. Uh . . .

MRS ELVSTED (*quietly, snuggling to* HEDDA). I'm so lucky, Hedda! Imagine, he calls me his inspiration.

HEDDA (*smiling at her*). Darling. Really?

LØVBORG. She has courage, Mrs Tesman. The courage that gets things done.

MRS ELVSTED. Me? Courage? No.

LØVBORG. The courage to fight. For her comrade in arms.

HEDDA. That courage. Ah. The kind –

LØVBORG. What kind?

HEDDA. – that lets one live. (*Change of tone.*) Thea, dearest, do have a glass of punch.

MRS ELVSTED. No thank you. I never drink alcohol.

HEDDA. Mr Løvborg? Surely.

LØVBORG. Thank you. No.

MRS ELVSTED. He doesn't either.

HEDDA (*looking steadily at him*). Not even for my sake?

LØVBORG. Sorry, no.

HEDDA (*lightly*). Oh dear. I've no power over you at all?

LØVBORG. Not where that's concerned.

HEDDA. I really think you should. For your own sake.

MRS ELVSTED. Hedda!

LØVBORG. What d'you mean?

HEDDA. Or rather, for other people's sake.

LØVBORG. Yes?

HEDDA. In case they think that you . . . can't trust yourself. Absolute trust.

MRS ELVSTED (*quietly*). Hedda. No.

LØVBORG. They can think what they like. They'll see.

MRS ELVSTED (*delighted*). That's right.

HEDDA. I could see, earlier. When Judge Brack –

LØVBORG. What did you see?

HEDDA. I saw how he smiled when you were afraid to go to that party.

LØVBORG. I preferred to stay here with you.

MRS ELVSTED. You see, Hedda.

HEDDA. The Judge couldn't see. I noticed him smiling, glancing at Tesman. Afraid, afraid to go to their harmless little party.

LØVBORG. Don't call me afraid.

HEDDA. Not me. Judge Brack. That's what he thought.

LØVBORG. He can think what he likes.

HEDDA. You're not going?

LØVBORG. I'm staying here with you and Thea.

MRS ELVSTED. He's staying, Hedda.

HEDDA (*smiling and nodding approvingly at* LØVBORG). A rock. A man of principle. Just what a man should be.

She turns to MRS ELVSTED *and pats her.*

Didn't I tell you so this morning, when you were so upset?

LØVBORG (*startled*). Upset?

MRS ELVSTED (*aghast*). Hedda!

HEDDA. Now you see for yourself. There's no need. No need for all this panic. (*Breaking off.*) Never mind. Let's change the subject.

LØVBORG (*insistently*). Mrs Tesman, what is all this?

MRS ELVSTED. Hedda, what are you saying? What are you doing? Oh God.

HEDDA. Shh! That tiresome Judge Brack is watching.

LØVBORG. Panic. About me.

MRS ELVSTED (*quietly, miserably*). Hedda, how could you?

LØVBORG *gazes at her a moment, grim-faced.*

LØVBORG. Comrades in arms. So much for trust.

MRS ELVSTED (*beseeching him*). Please, my dear, please listen.

LØVBORG *snatches up a glass of punch.*

LØVBORG (*quietly, intensely*). Darling, your health.

He drains the glass and takes another.

MRS ELVSTED (*low*). You planned this, Hedda.

HEDDA. You're crazy. Planned?

LØVBORG. Mrs Tesman, your health. Thank you for the truth. To truth!

He drains the glass and refills it. HEDDA *puts a hand on his arm.*

HEDDA. No more for now. Don't forget, you're going out to dinner.

MRS ELVSTED. No, no, no.

HEDDA. Shh! They can see you.

LØVBORG (*putting down the glass*). Your turn, Thea. The truth.

MRS ELVSTED. Yes.

LØVBORG. Does your husband know you followed me?

MRS ELVSTED (*wringing her hands*). Hedda, d'you hear what he's asking me?

LØVBORG. Did you plan this together? You and he? That you'd come after me, spy on me? Was it his idea? Of course it was! He needed me to help in the office. An extra hand at cards!

MRS ELVSTED (*low, anguished*). Ejlert, Ejlert.

LØVBORG *seizes and fills a glass.*

LØVBORG. His health too! His Honour's health!

HEDDA (*checking him*). No more now. Don't forget Tesman. You're going to read him your book.

LØVBORG (*calmly, putting down the glass*). I'm sorry, Thea. I was a fool. Taking it like this. My darling, my comrade in arms, don't worry. Don't be afraid for me. You'll see, they'll all see. I fell before, but now . . . I'm up again. Dearest Thea, all thanks to you.

MRS ELVSTED (*overjoyed*). Thank God, thank God.

BRACK *has meantime looked at his watch, and now he and TESMAN come in from the inner room. BRACK takes his hat and coat.*

BRACK. Well, Mrs Tesman. It's time.

HEDDA. Yes, time.

LØVBORG (*getting up*). Time for me as well.

MRS ELVSTED (*low, beseeching*). Ejlert, don't.

HEDDA (*pinching her arm*). They can hear you.

MRS ELVSTED (*a little shriek*). Ow.

LØVBORG (*to BRACK*). Your generous invitation.

BRACK. You're coming?

LØVBORG. Please. If I may.

BRACK. Splendid.

LØVBORG *puts his manuscript in his pocket.*

LØVBORG (*to TESMAN*). I've one or two things to show you before I send it off.

TESMAN. Wonderful. Hedda, darling, how will you get Mrs Elvsted home?

HEDDA. We'll find a way.

LØVBORG (*looking at the women*). Mrs Elvsted? I'll fetch her. No question. I'll come and fetch her. (*Going closer.*) Mrs Tesman, about ten o'clock?

HEDDA. Perfect.

TESMAN. Splendid. Excellent. But you mustn't expect me so early, Hedda.

HEDDA. My dear man, stay as long as you like.

MRS ELVSTED (*with forced calm*). Mr Løvborg, I'll wait here till you come.

LØVBORG (*hat in hand*). Mrs Elvsted, excellent.

BRACK. So, gentlemen, the carnival begins! I hope it'll be . . . 'jolly', as a certain charming lady puts it.

HEDDA. I wish a certain charming lady could be there, invisible –

BRACK. Why invisible?

HEDDA. Why Your Honour, to hear some of your . . . jollity uncensored.

BRACK (*laughing*). It's not for charming ladies' ears.

TESMAN (*laughing too*). It certainly isn't, Hedda.

BRACK. Ladies, good afternoon.

LØVBORG (*bowing*). Till ten o'clock.

BRACK, LØVBORG *and* TESMAN *go out by the hall. At the same time,* BERTA *comes from the inner room with a lighted lamp, puts it on the table and exit as she came in.* MRS ELVSTED *has got up and is pacing restlessly.*

MRS ELVSTED. Hedda, Hedda, what's going to happen?

HEDDA. At ten o'clock, he'll be here. I see him. With vine leaves in his hair. Flushed, confident –

MRS ELVSTED. Oh if only –

HEDDA. He'll have proved himself. In control of himself again. He'll be free, then, forever free.

MRS ELVSTED. God send him so.

HEDDA. He must be. Will be. (*Going to her.*) You doubt him if you like. I believe in him. And now, we'll see.

MRS ELVSTED. Hedda, what is it you want from this?

HEDDA. For once in my life, I want to control another human being's fate.

MRS ELVSTED. But you do.

HEDDA. No I don't.

MRS ELVSTED. Your husband.

HEDDA. If I did . . . You don't know how poor I am. And you, you: promised such riches!

She hugs her affectionately.

I think I'll burn your hair off after all.

MRS ELVSTED. Let me go! Hedda! You're frightening me.

BERTA (*at the door*). Tea's laid in the dining-room, madam.

HEDDA. We're coming.

MRS ELVSTED. No, no! I want to go home. Home, now!

HEDDA. What a goose you are. First, you'll have some tea. Then, at ten o'clock, Ejlert Løvborg will be here . . . with vine leaves in his hair.

She all but drags her into the inner room.

ACT THREE

The scene is the same. The curtains have been drawn over the main doorway and the screen door to the garden. A lighted lamp is on the table, shaded and half turned down. The stove door is open, and the dying embers of a fire can be seen. MRS ELVSTED is lying back in an armchair next to the stove, with her feet on a stool. HEDDA is asleep on the sofa, fully dressed and covered by a rug. After a moment, MRS ELVSTED sits up and listens intently. Then she sinks wearily back.

MRS ELVSTED (*whimpering pitifully*). Still no. Oh God, still no.

BERTA *tiptoes in through the hall door with a letter.* MRS ELVSTED *turns and whispers eagerly:*

News? Something's happened?

BERTA (*in a low voice*). A servant just came with this.

MRS ELVSTED (*eagerly, holding out her hand*). A letter! Give it to me.

BERTA. I can't, madam. It's for Doctor Tesman.

MRS ELVSTED. Oh.

BERTA. Miss Tesman's maid brought it. I'll leave it on the table.

MRS ELVSTED. Yes.

BERTA *puts the letter on the table.*

BERTA. The lamp's smoking. I ought to put it out.

MRS ELVSTED. Yes. Please. It'll soon be dawn.

BERTA (*putting out the lamp*). It is dawn, madam.

MRS ELVSTED. Broad daylight! And they're still not home.

BERTA. I expected this.

MRS ELVSTED. Expected it?

BERTA. As soon as I knew that a certain person had come back to town . . . And then when he went off with them . . . We all know that gentleman's reputation.

MRS ELVSTED. Not so loud. You'll waken Mrs Tesman.

BERTA (*looking at the sofa and sighing*). Yes. Let the poor soul sleep. Should I make up the stove?

MRS ELVSTED. Not on my account, thank you.

BERTA. Yes madam.

She leaves quietly through the hall. The noise of the door closing wakens HEDDA.

HEDDA. What's that?

MRS ELVSTED. Just Berta.

HEDDA (*looking round*). Here . . . Oh yes.

She sits up, stretches and rubs her eyes.

What time is it, Thea?

MRS ELVSTED (*looking at her watch*). Just after seven.

HEDDA. When did Tesman come in?

MRS ELVSTED. He didn't.

HEDDA. Didn't?

MRS ELVSTED (*getting up*). No one did.

HEDDA. After we sat up and waited till four o'clock!

MRS ELVSTED (*wringing her hands*). I waited so hard for him.

HEDDA (*smothering a yawn*). We needn't have bothered.

MRS ELVSTED. Did you sleep at all?

HEDDA. Yes thank you. Very well. Did you?

MRS ELVSTED. Not a wink. I couldn't, Hedda.

HEDDA gets up and goes to her.

HEDDA. Don't worry. It's all right. It's perfectly clear what happened.

MRS ELVSTED. What d'you mean?

HEDDA. It's obvious. They stayed very late at Judge Brack's –

MRS ELVSTED. Oh. Yes. Even so –

HEDDA. – and Jørgen decided not to waken the whole household, ringing the bell in the middle of the night. (*With a laugh.*) In any case, perhaps he wasn't fit to be seen. Rather a heavy night . . .

MRS ELVSTED. But Hedda, where did he go instead?

HEDDA. The aunts, of course. His old room. They keep it just as it was. He'll have gone there to sleep.

MRS ELVSTED. He can't have done. A note's just come from Miss Tesman. On the table, there.

HEDDA. Hm.

She looks at the letter.

Aunt Julia's writing. Well, he'll still be at Judge Brack's. Ejlert Løvborg too. He'll be sitting there, reading his book to him . . . with vine leaves in his hair.

MRS ELVSTED. You're just saying that, Hedda. You don't believe it; you're just saying it.

HEDDA. You are a goose.

MRS ELVSTED. I'm sorry.

HEDDA. You look worn out.

MRS ELVSTED. I am.

HEDDA. Well then, do as I say. Go to my room, lie down, take a nap.

MRS ELVSTED. I won't sleep.

HEDDA. You will if you try.

MRS ELVSTED. Your husband'll be home any minute. And I've got to know –

HEDDA. As soon as he comes, I'll tell you.

MRS ELVSTED. D'you promise, Hedda?

HEDDA. Cross my heart. Meantime, go in and sleep.

MRS ELVSTED. Yes. Thank you.

She goes in through the inner room. HEDDA *goes to the screen door and draws the curtains. Daylight fills the room. She takes a hand mirror from the writing desk and straightens her hair. Then she goes to the bellpull by the hall door and rings. After a short pause,* BERTA *comes to the door.*

BERTA. Yes, madam?

HEDDA. Make up the stove, will you? I'm shivering.

BERTA. Bless you, it'll be warm in no time.

She rakes the stove and puts in fresh wood. Then she stops and listens.

There's someone at the front door, madam.

HEDDA. You answer it. I'll see to the stove.

BERTA. It'll soon burn up.

She goes out through the hall. HEDDA *kneels on a footstool and feeds the stove. After a short pause,* TESMAN *comes in from the hall. He looks exhausted and anxious. He tiptoes across the room to the main door and puts out a hand to draw the curtains.*

HEDDA (*at the stove, without looking up*). Good morning.

TESMAN (*turning*). Hedda!

He goes to her.

What on Earth . . . ? You're up early.

HEDDA. So I am.

TESMAN. I was sure you'd be fast asleep.

HEDDA. Not so loud. Mrs Elvsted's asleep in there.

TESMAN. She spent the night here?

HEDDA. No one came to take her home.

TESMAN. No, that's right.

HEDDA *closes the stove door and stands up.*

HEDDA. How was it at Judge Brack's? Was it . . . jolly?

TESMAN. You were worried about me.

HEDDA. I just asked if it was jolly.

TESMAN. Oh, yes. Especially to begin with, so far as I was concerned. That's when Ejlert read to me. We were an hour too early. Brack had a hundred things to do. So Ejlert read.

HEDDA *sits, right of the table.*

HEDDA. Yes. Tell me –

TESMAN *sits on a stool by the stove.*

TESMAN. Hedda, you can't imagine what it's like, his book. One of the most amazing ever written.

HEDDA. I'm really not interested.

TESMAN. And d'you know, Hedda, when he'd finished . . .
    I have to admit it . . . I felt awful. Awful.

HEDDA. I don't understand.

TESMAN. I sat there feeling jealous. That Ejlert could write
    like that. Jealous, Hedda!

HEDDA. I heard you.

TESMAN. And then to think that a man like him . . . so
    gifted . . . should be so . . . beyond reach.

HEDDA. Beyond reach? Of what – mediocrity?

TESMAN. Of control! Control!

HEDDA. What d'you mean? What happened?

TESMAN. It was . . . well, it was an orgy, Hedda.

HEDDA. Did he have vine leaves in his hair?

TESMAN. I didn't see any. He made a rambling speech about
    the woman who'd inspired him. His Muse, he called her.

HEDDA. Did he mention her name?

TESMAN. No. But I'm sure he meant Mrs Elvsted. No smoke
    without fire!

HEDDA. Mm. Where did you leave him?

TESMAN. On the way here. We left the party – the few that
    were left – all together. Brack came out with us: he wanted
    some fresh air. The end of it was, we all saw Ejlert home.
    He was . . . well gone.

HEDDA. Well gone.

TESMAN. But this is the amazing part, Hedda. Or the
    depressing part, rather. I'm embarrassed to tell it . . . for
    Ejlert's sake.

HEDDA. Tell what?

TESMAN. We were walking along. I was a little behind the others. A couple of minutes. More or less . . .

HEDDA. For Heaven's sake!

TESMAN. I was hurrying to catch them up – and there, by the side of the road . . . what d'you think?

HEDDA. I don't know. What?

TESMAN. Hedda, don't breathe a word. To anyone. Promise. For Ejlert's sake.

He takes a large envelope from his coat pocket.

I found . . . this.

HEDDA. That's the package he brought here yesterday.

TESMAN. His priceless, irreplaceable manuscript. He lost it, and he didn't even notice. Just think what a tragedy –

HEDDA. Why didn't you give it him right away?

TESMAN. I couldn't. The state he was in.

HEDDA. Did you tell anyone else you'd found it?

TESMAN. I didn't want to. For Ejlert's sake.

HEDDA. So you've got Ejlert Løvborg's book, and no one knows?

TESMAN. That's right. And no one must know, either.

HEDDA. What did you say to him?

TESMAN. Nothing. I didn't have a chance. By the time we got to the centre of town, he and one or two others had vanished. Vanished.

HEDDA. So they must have seen him home.

TESMAN. Exactly. And Brack went home as well.

HEDDA. And since then: what have you been doing?

TESMAN. A few of us took someone else home, someone else who was . . . We had a cup of coffee – Ha! breakfast in the middle of the night! I'll just take a nap . . . I'll wait till poor Ejlert's slept it off . . . then I'll go round and give him this.

HEDDA (*reaching for the envelope*). No, keep it. I mean, for a little longer. Let me read it first.

TESMAN. Darling, I can't. I can't.

HEDDA. Why not?

TESMAN. Think what he'll be like when he wakes up and finds he's lost it. He'll be frantic. This is the only copy. There isn't another.

HEDDA (*with a long look at him*). Can't this sort of thing be written again? A second version?

TESMAN. I shouldn't think so. Inspiration –

HEDDA. Ah well. (*Casually.*) I nearly forgot. There's a letter.

TESMAN. Pardon?

HEDDA (*pointing*). It came earlier.

TESMAN. From Aunt Julia. What can it be?

He puts LØVBORG's *envelope on the other footstool, opens the letter, reads and starts.*

Hedda! She says that poor Aunt Rina's . . . at death's door.

HEDDA. Are you surprised?

TESMAN. And if I want to see her again, I'd better hurry. I'll run –

HEDDA (*lightly*). Run?

TESMAN. Hedda, darling, if only you'd . . . if only you'd come too. Come too.

HEDDA (*getting up; in a weary, dismissive tone*). No. Don't ask.
I can't bear sick people, dead people. They're . . . ugly.

TESMAN. Yes. (*Fretting.*) My hat . . . my coat . . . ? In the
hall. Oh Hedda, I hope I'm not too late. Too late . . .

HEDDA. You'd better run.

Enter BERTA *from the hall.*

BERTA. His Honour the Judge is here. Shall I show him in?

TESMAN. Now of all times! I can't see him now.

HEDDA. But I can. (*To* BERTA.) Show the gentleman in.
(*Urgent whisper, to* TESMAN.) The package!

She takes it from the stool.

TESMAN. Yes. Give it me.

HEDDA. It's all right. I'll keep it for you. Go.

She puts the envelope on one of the shelves of the writing-desk.
TESMAN *stands there flustered, struggling with his gloves. Enter*
BRACK *from the hall.*

HEDDA (*nodding to him*). You are an early bird.

BRACK. You think so? (*To* TESMAN.) You on your way as
well?

TESMAN. No choice. My aunts. Poor Aunt Rina, she's at
death's door.

BRACK. Good Lord. Don't let me stop you.

TESMAN. Yes, excuse me, I really must . . . Goodbye,
goodbye.

Exit through the hall.

HEDDA (*going to* BRACK). Quite a night, last night, Your
Honour. Rather more than 'jolly'.

BRACK. Dear Mrs Tesman, I haven't even changed.

HEDDA. You too?

BRACK. Me too. But what's Tesman been telling you?

HEDDA. Nothing very interesting. They went somewhere for coffee.

BRACK. I know about the coffee. Ejlert Løvborg wasn't with them?

HEDDA. They saw him home earlier.

BRACK. Tesman?

HEDDA. A couple of others. Or so he said.

BRACK (*smiling*). Good, honest Tesman.

HEDDA. Absolutely. But what's all this about?

BRACK. You guessed: there's more than meets the eye.

HEDDA. Well, let's sit down. Tell your tale in comfort.

She sits left of the table. BRACK *sits at its long side next to her.*

Go on.

BRACK. It was just as well I checked that my guests got home last night. Or to be exact, some of my guests.

HEDDA. Including, perhaps . . . Ejlert Løvborg?

BRACK. I'm afraid so.

HEDDA. I'm listening.

BRACK. Mrs Tesman, d'you know where he and a couple of the others spent the rest of last night?

HEDDA. Tell me – if it can be told.

BRACK. It can be told. They ended up at a . . . very lively soirée.

HEDDA. Jolly?

BRACK. None jollier.

HEDDA. Go on. Please.

BRACK. Løvborg had been invited. Earlier. I knew that. But he'd refused. Said he'd turned over a new leaf. As you know.

HEDDA. Up at the Elvsteds'. But still he went?

BRACK. Exactly. The idea . . . came to him at my house.

HEDDA. I heard he was 'inspired'.

BRACK. Raging 'inspired'. Whatever it was, he changed his mind about the other invitation. We men aren't always as firm in our resolve as we like to think.

HEDDA. Except for yourself, Your Honour. So Løvborg –

BRACK. To cut it short, he finally reached harbour at Mamzelle Diana's.

HEDDA. Mamzelle Diana's?

BRACK. It was her soirée. For a chosen circle of . . . lady friends and admirers.

HEDDA. She's the one with red hair?

BRACK. Yes.

HEDDA. A kind of . . . singer?

BRACK. Kind of singer, kind of hunter – at least, of men. You've obviously heard of her. Ejlert Løvborg was one of her most devoted followers, in his heyday.

HEDDA. But what happened?

BRACK. A scene. Mamzelle Diana soon moved from hugs to blows.

HEDDA. Against Løvborg?

BRACK. He swore that she or her lady friends had robbed him. His wallet. Other things. He made a spectacular fuss.

HEDDA. Then what?

BRACK. A wrestling-match. Ladies *and* gentlemen. Fortunately, at this point the police arrived.

HEDDA. The police?

BRACK. Things look hot for Master Løvborg. Master fool!

HEDDA. What d'you mean?

BRACK. He resisted. Fiercely. Boxed one constable's ears. Ripped his uniform. So he ended up at the station too.

HEDDA. Who told you all this?

BRACK. The police.

HEDDA (*gazing straight ahead*). So that's how it was. No vine leaves.

BRACK. Vine leaves?

HEDDA (*change of tone*). Your Honour, tell me. Why do you care so much what Ejlert Løvborg did?

BRACK. For one thing, my position. If it comes out at the trial that he began at my house.

HEDDA. There's going to be a trial?

BRACK. So they say. Maybe so, maybe not. In any case, as a friend of the family, I felt I really ought to tell you and Tesman exactly what went on last night.

HEDDA. But why?

BRACK. I've a feeling he may use you as a kind of . . . screen.

HEDDA. I don't understand.

BRACK. For heaven's sake! Mrs Tesman, we're none of us blind. I'm telling you, Mrs Elvsted won't be hurrying out of town.

HEDDA. Ridiculous! If there is anything between them, there are a dozen other places they can meet.

BRACK. Nowhere else respectable. Every respectable door will be closed to Løvborg now.

HEDDA. Including mine, you're suggesting?

BRACK. I have to tell you I'd be most displeased to find him admitted here. To find him making his way, uninvited, unwanted –

HEDDA. Into the triangle?

BRACK. It would be like losing one's home.

HEDDA (*smiling at him*). Just one cock of the walk, you mean.

BRACK (*nodding slowly and lowering his voice*). Exactly. That's exactly what I mean. And what I'll fight for, any way I can.

HEDDA (*no longer smiling*). You're a dangerous man, when the going gets rough.

BRACK. You think so?

HEDDA. I'm beginning to. And I'm heartily glad you've got no hold or power over me at all.

BRACK (*laughing ambiguously*). You may be right. But who knows, Mrs Tesman? One day I may find both.

HEDDA. Your Honour, are you threatening me?

BRACK (*getting up*). Not in the least. The triangle depends for its strength entirely on free will.

HEDDA. Exactly.

BRACK. Well, I've said what I came to say. I'll be getting home again. Good morning, Mrs Tesman.

He goes to the screen door.

HEDDA (*getting up*). You're going through the garden?

BRACK. It's quicker.

HEDDA. And a back way, too.

BRACK. I've nothing against back ways. Sometimes they're quite . . . exciting.

HEDDA. For example, when someone's shooting?

BRACK (*laughing, from the doorway*). Whoever shoots the cock of the walk?

HEDDA (*laughing*). Especially when it's the only one.

Still laughing, they nod goodbye.

BRACK *goes, and* HEDDA *closes the door behind him. She stands for a moment looking out. Then she goes to the main door, peeps through the curtains, and takes* LØVBORG's *envelope from the writing-desk. She is just about to open it when* BERTA's *raised voice is heard in the hall.* HEDDA *turns and listens, then quickly locks the envelope in a drawer and puts the key on the inkstand.* LØVBORG *throws open the door from the hall and comes in. He is wearing an overcoat and carrying his hat. He seems beside himself with worry.*

LØVBORG (*to* BERTA, *behind him in the hall*). Get out of the way. I'm going in.

He closes the door, turns, sees HEDDA *by the writing-desk, controls himself and bows.*

HEDDA. My dear Mr Løvborg, you're a little late to be fetching Thea.

LØVBORG. Or a little early to be making social calls. Do excuse me.

HEDDA. How did you know she'd still be here?

LØVBORG. They told me at her lodgings that she'd been out all night.

HEDDA *goes to the table.*

HEDDA. And when they told you, did you notice anything about them?

LØVBORG (*with an enquiring look*). Notice anything?

HEDDA. As if they had . . . views about it?

LØVBORG (*suddenly understanding*). Yes, that's true too. I'm dragging her down with me. Tch, I didn't notice anything. Is Jørgen up?

HEDDA. I don't think so.

LØVBORG. When did he come home?

HEDDA. Late.

LØVBORG. Did he tell you anything?

HEDDA. What a jolly evening you all had at His Honour's.

LØVBORG. Nothing else?

HEDDA. I don't think so. I wasn't really awake.

Enter MRS ELVSTED *through the curtained rear doors. She runs to him.*

MRS ELVSTED. Ejlert! At last!

LØVBORG. At last. Too late.

MRS ELVSTED (*with a wild look at him*). What d'you mean, too late?

LØVBORG. Too late for me. All of it. Finished.

MRS ELVSTED. Don't say that.

LØVBORG. You'll say it yourself when you hear –

MRS ELVSTED. I won't hear.

HEDDA. Would you like to talk to her in private? If you like, I'll –

LØVBORG. No. Stay. Please.

MRS ELVSTED. I won't hear. I won't.

LØVBORG. I don't mean last night.

MRS ELVSTED. What then?

LØVBORG. Our . . . ways must part.

MRS ELVSTED. Part!

HEDDA (*blurted*). I knew it!

LØVBORG. Thea, I don't need you any more.

MRS ELVSTED. How can you say that? Don't need me! You mean I can't go on helping you? We can't still work together?

LØVBORG. I shan't be working now.

MRS ELVSTED (*in despair*). And my life now? What use is that?

LØVBORG. You have to try to live as if you'd never met me.

MRS ELVSTED. How can I do that?

LØVBORG. Try, Thea. Go home –

MRS ELVSTED (*violently*). I won't. Never again! I'll be where you are. I won't be sent away. I'll stay here. When the book comes out, I'll be at your side.

HEDDA (*low, agog*). Aha. The book.

LØVBORG (*looking at her*). Our book. Mine, and Thea's. For that's what it is.

MRS ELVSTED. It is, it is. That's why I've the right to be with you then, when it comes out. To see them showering you with respect again, with honour. And the pleasure, the pleasure – to share that too.

LØVBORG. Thea, our book will never come out.

HEDDA. Ah!

MRS ELVSTED. What d'you mean?

LØVBORG. It can't.

MRS ELVSTED (*with terrified foreboding*). Ejlert! What have you done with the manuscript?

HEDDA (*looking narrowly at him*). That's right. The manuscript.

LØVBORG. Don't ask me.

MRS ELVSTED. Of course I'll ask. I've a right to know. Now.

LØVBORG. The manuscript. Well. I've torn it to a thousand pieces.

MRS ELVSTED (*shrieking*). No. No.

HEDDA (*involuntarily*). But that's –

LØVBORG (*looking at her*). Not true, you mean?

HEDDA (*recovering*). Oh. True. Of course. If you say so. It seemed . . . astounding.

LØVBORG. Still true.

MRS ELVSTED (*wringing her hands*). Oh no. Oh God. His own work, Hedda. His own work, to pieces.

LØVBORG. His life. I've torn my life to pieces. So why not my life's work too?

MRS ELVSTED. You did this last night.

LØVBORG. I keep telling you. A thousand pieces. And threw them in the fjord. Into deep, clean sea. Let them drift there. Drift in the winds, the waves. Then sink. Deeper, deeper. As I shall, Thea.

MRS ELVSTED. Ejlert, what you've done, to this book – all my life I – it's as if you'd killed a child.

LØVBORG. A child. Yes. I've killed a child.

MRS ELVSTED. It was my child too. How could you?

HEDDA (*almost inaudible*). Oh, the child . . .

MRS ELVSTED (*breathing heavily*). It's over. I'll go now, Hedda.

HEDDA. Back home?

MRS ELVSTED. I don't know what I'll do.

Exit through the hall. HEDDA *stands there. Pause.*

HEDDA. Mr Løvborg, I take it you're not seeing her home.

LØVBORG. In broad daylight? You want people to see her with me?

HEDDA. Naturally, I don't know what else went on last night. Something . . . irrevocable?

LØVBORG. Last night won't be the last. I know. And I don't want to live like that. Not again. I squared up to life . . . took it by the throat. She's smashed that.

HEDDA (*looking straight ahead*). Such a silly little goose, and she's changed another human being's destiny. (*To him.*) Even so, you can't be so heartless to her.

LØVBORG. Don't call it heartless.

HEDDA. Not heartless? You gave her . . . you filled her soul . . . and then you burst it apart.

LØVBORG. Hedda, listen.

HEDDA. I'm listening.

LØVBORG. First, promise, give me your word. What I tell you now, Thea must never know.

HEDDA. I promise.

LØVBORG. Thank you. Then – it wasn't true, the tale I told before.

HEDDA. The manuscript?

LØVBORG. I didn't tear it to pieces. Didn't throw it in the fjord.

HEDDA. Good gracious. Where is it, then?

LØVBORG. Destroyed. Just the same, destroyed. Entirely.

HEDDA. I don't understand.

LØVBORG. Thea said . . . what I'd done . . . to her it was like murdering a child.

HEDDA. That's what she said.

LØVBORG. For a father to kill his child . . . that's not the worst he can do.

HEDDA. It isn't?

LØVBORG. I didn't want Thea to hear the worst.

HEDDA. What is this worst?

LØVBORG. Imagine a father, Hedda, a husband . . . next morning . . . after a night of . . . wildness, recklessness . . . went home to his child's mother and said, 'I went there and there. I took the child. There and there. And I lost him. Lost him. Devil knows who's got him now. Who's got their hands on him.'

HEDDA. This was a book, that's all.

LØVBORG. Thea's soul was in that book.

HEDDA. Yes.

LØVBORG. You see why there's no future now? For her and me?

HEDDA. What are you going to do?

LØVBORG. Nothing. Finish it, somehow. Now.

HEDDA (*one step closer*). Listen, Ejlert Løvborg . . . Try to . . . Make it . . . beautiful.

LØVBORG. Beautiful?

He smiles.

With vine leaves in one's hair. D'you remember . . . ?

HEDDA. Not vine leaves now. But still, beautiful. For once! Goodbye. Go, now. Don't come again.

LØVBORG. Goodbye, Mrs Tesman. My regards to Doctor Tesman.

He makes to leave.

HEDDA. Wait. I want you to have . . . a keepsake.

She goes to the writing-desk, opens the gun-case, and gives him one of the pistols.

LØVBORG (*looking at her*). A . . . keepsake.

HEDDA (*nodding slowly*). Don't you recognise it? It was aimed at you, once.

LØVBORG. You should have used it then.

HEDDA. You use it now.

LØVBORG *puts the pistol in his breast pocket.*

LØVBORG. Thank you.

HEDDA. Ejlert Løvborg, beautiful. Promise me that.

LØVBORG. Goodbye, Hedda Gabler.

Exit through the hall. HEDDA *listens a moment at the door. Then she goes to the writing-desk, takes out the manuscript in its envelope, pulls out a page or two and looks at them. She goes to sit in the armchair by the stove. The envelope is in her lap. Pause. Then she opens the stove door and the envelope, and begins stuffing the pages into the stove.*

HEDDA (*whispering to herself*). Look, Thea. I'm burning your baby, Thea. Little curly-hair!

Stuffing more pages in.

Your baby . . . yours and his.

Stuffing the whole manuscript in.

The baby. Burning the baby.

ACT FOUR

The scene is the same. Evening. The main room is in darkness. The inner room is lit by a lamp hanging over the table. The curtains before the screen door are drawn. HEDDA, in black, is pacing the floor in the dark room. She goes into the inner room and out of sight, left. We hear a chord or two on the piano before she returns to the main room. BERTA brings a lighted lamp right from the inner room, and puts it on the table in front of the corner sofa. Her eyes are red and she has black ribbons in her cap. She slips quietly out right. HEDDA goes to the screen door, moves the curtain a little aside and looks out into the darkness. After a short pause, MISS TESMAN comes in from the hall. She is dressed in black, with hat and veil. HEDDA goes to her, hand outstretched.

MISS TESMAN. Dear Hedda, I come to you all in black. My poor sister's torments are over at last.

HEDDA. As you can see, I know already. Jørgen sent a note.

MISS TESMAN. He said he would. But all the same I thought: I ought to go myself, to Hedda, in the house of life, and break the sad news in person.

HEDDA. Very kind.

MISS TESMAN. Ah, Rina should have stayed. Not passed away now. This is no time for grief in Hedda's house.

HEDDA (*changing the subject*). A peaceful death?

MISS TESMAN. Peaceful . . . beautiful. She had the inexpressible pleasure of seeing Jørgen once more, just before the end. To say goodbye . . . He's not back yet?

HEDDA. He said in the note that he might be some time. Do sit down.

MISS TESMAN. Dear, sweet Hedda, no. Thank you. I wish I could. But there's so little time. She must be prepared, made ready, as best I can. When she goes to her grave, she must look her best.

HEDDA. Is there anything I can do?

MISS TESMAN. No, no. That's not for Hedda Tesman now. Not to do, not even to think about. At a time like this? No, no.

HEDDA. Thoughts. Who can control them?

MISS TESMAN (*running on*). Lord knows, that's how things are. At home, we'll be sewing Rina's shroud. And there'll be sewing here, too. Very soon, I'm sure. Of a very different kind, God send it so.

Enter TESMAN *from the hall.*

HEDDA. Thank God you're here at last.

TESMAN. Aunt Julia! Here, with Hedda! Here!

MISS TESMAN. I was just going. Darling boy. Have you done everything you promised?

TESMAN. Forgotten some of it, I'm afraid. I'll pop round tomorrow, see you then. My head's in such a whirl today, I can't keep my thoughts in order.

MISS TESMAN. Darling Jørgen, you mustn't take it this way.

TESMAN. How, then?

MISS TESMAN. You must be happy in your tears. Happy. As I am.

TESMAN. Oh, for Aunt Rina, you mean?

HEDDA. It'll be lonely for you now, Miss Tesman.

MISS TESMAN. For a day or two. But not for long, I hope.
  Poor Rina's little room won't stand empty long.

TESMAN. Are you moving someone in?

MISS TESMAN. There's always some poor, sick soul to nurse,
  to care for. Alas.

HEDDA. You'll take on that cross again?

MISS TESMAN. God bless you, child, why should you think
  it was a cross?

HEDDA. I mean, this time, a stranger −

MISS TESMAN. With sick people, one soon makes friends. I
  must have someone to live for. And here: God be praised,
  there may be one or two things here, too, for an old aunt
  to do.

HEDDA. Leave us out of −

TESMAN. We could be so happy together, the three of us.
  I mean if −

HEDDA. If?

TESMAN (*uneasily*). Nothing. It'll be all right. Let's hope so.
  Hope so.

MISS TESMAN. Well, I expect you've lots to talk about.
  (*Smiling.*) Hedda may even have news for you, Jørgen.
  Goodbye. I'll get back to Rina. (*At the door.*) It's so hard to
  take in. She's with me now, Rina, and with poor dear
  Jochum too.

TESMAN. Imagine that, Aunt Julia. Imagine.

  Exit MISS TESMAN *through the hall.* HEDDA *is following*
  TESMAN *with cold, sharp eyes.*

HEDDA. You're more upset by this death than she is.

TESMAN. It's not just Aunt Rina's death. It's Ejlert.

HEDDA (*quickly*). What about him?

TESMAN. I popped round this afternoon to tell him the manuscript was safe and sound.

HEDDA. Wasn't he there?

TESMAN. He was out. But I met Mrs Elvsted, and she said he came here this morning, early.

HEDDA. You just missed him.

TESMAN. Apparently he said he'd torn that book to pieces.

HEDDA. He did say that.

TESMAN. He must have been beside himself. I suppose you didn't like to give it back to him.

HEDDA. He didn't take it.

TESMAN. You told him we had it?

HEDDA. No. (*Quickly.*) Did you tell Mrs Elvsted?

TESMAN. I didn't want to do that. But you could've told him. The state he's in – what if he . . . hurts himself? Give me the manuscript, Hedda. I'll take it round right now. Where is it?

HEDDA (*like stone, leaning against the chair*). It's gone. I haven't got it.

TESMAN. Haven't got it? What on Earth d'you mean?

HEDDA. I burned it. All of it.

TESMAN (*horror-struck*). You burned Ejlert's manuscript?

HEDDA. Stop shouting. Berta will hear you.

TESMAN. God in heaven. Burned. You can't –

HEDDA. I can; I did.

TESMAN. D'you realise what you've done? Destroying lost property – it's a criminal act. Ask Brack.

HEDDA. Don't tell anyone, then. Not Brack, not anyone.

TESMAN. But how could you do it? How could you, Hedda?

HEDDA (*hiding a smile*). I did it for you, Jørgen.

TESMAN. For me!

HEDDA. You came home this morning. You said he'd read to you.

TESMAN. Yes.

HEDDA. And you were jealous. You said.

TESMAN. I didn't mean it literally.

HEDDA. That's not the point. I still couldn't bear it: the idea of someone else putting you in the shade.

TESMAN (*in an outburst: half unsure, half glad*). Hedda? Is this true? What you're saying . . . ? I . . . you've never shown your love like this before. Never.

HEDDA. You might as well know. The thing is –

She breaks off.

Oh, ask Aunt Julia. She'll explain.

TESMAN. I . . . I think I know. (*Clasping his hands.*) Oh God, oh God, is it really true?

HEDDA. Stop shouting. Berta will hear you.

TESMAN (*laughing, overcome with happiness*). Berta! Oh, Hedda, you're priceless! Berta! It's Berta! I'll tell her myself.

HEDDA (*clenching her fists in despair*). I can't stand this. I can't stand any more.

TESMAN. Stand what, Hedda?

HEDDA (*cold, controlled*). All this . . . fuss.

TESMAN. But I'm delighted, I'm overjoyed! Well, perhaps, not a word to Berta.

HEDDA. Why not? Why ever not?

TESMAN. Not now, this minute. But Aunt Julia must be told. And you've started to call me Jørgen. Jørgen! She'll be so happy, Aunt Julia, so happy.

HEDDA. To hear that I burned Ejlert Løvborg's book – for you?

TESMAN. No, well. Not the book. But that you burn for me, Hedda – that's what Aunt Julia needs to know. Hedda, darling, is this what all young wives are like?

HEDDA. You could ask Aunt Julia that as well.

TESMAN. Good idea. I will. (*Worried and hesitant again*). Even so, that manuscript. Poor Ejlert. Even so.

MRS ELVSTED, *dressed as on her first visit, with hat and coat, comes in from the hall. She greets them quickly and with agitation.*

MRS ELVSTED. Hedda, I'm sorry to come again so soon –

HEDDA. Thea, what is it?

TESMAN. Ejlert Løvborg? Something new?

MRS ELVSTED. I'm afraid. I think something terrible's happened.

HEDDA (*takes her by the arm*). You think so.

TESMAN. Good heavens, Mrs Elvsted, what makes you think that?

MRS ELVSTED. When I got back to the boarding house just now, they were talking about him. There are rumours about him everywhere!

TESMAN. I thought he went straight home to bed.

HEDDA. In the boarding house – what were they saying?

MES ELVSTED. Nothing definite. Not to me, anyway. Either they didn't know, or . . . they stopped talking when they saw me. I didn't dare ask.

TESMAN (*pacing restlessly*). Let's hope . . . let's hope you heard wrong, Mrs Elvsted.

MES ELVSTED. It was him they were talking about. I'm sure it was. I'm sure someone mentioned the hospital –

TESMAN. Hospital!

HEDDA. They can't have.

MRS ELVSTED. I was so terrified for him. I went to his lodgings and asked for him there.

HEDDA. Thea! You dared do that?

MRS ELVSTED. What else could I do? Not knowing – I couldn't bear it.

TESMAN. He wasn't there?

MRS ELVSTED. They knew nothing about him. He hadn't been home since yesterday afternoon, they said.

TESMAN. Yesterday! What do they mean?

MRS ELVSTED. There's only one explanation: something dreadful's happened.

TESMAN. Hedda, shall I go . . . make inquiries?

HEDDA. No. No. Don't get involved.

BERTA *opens the hall door, and* BRACK *comes in. She closes the door behind him. He looks grave, and greets them solemnly.*

TESMAN. Brack. It's you. It's you.

BRACK. I had to see you this evening.

TESMAN. I see from your face, you've heard Aunt Julia's sad news.

BRACK. That too.

TESMAN. A tragedy.

BRACK. Depends how you look at it.

TESMAN (*with an enquiring look*). Something else?

HEDDA (*intent*). Judge Brack, another tragedy?

TESMAN. Depends how you look at it, Mrs Tesman.

MRS ELVSTED (*unable to contain herself*). It's about Ejlert Løvborg.

BRACK (*glancing at her*). Why d'you say that? Mrs Elvsted? You've heard something already?

MRS ELVSTED (*confused*). No . . . I . . . no . . .

TESMAN. Good Heavens, tell us!

BRACK (*shrugging*). I'm sorry to say . . . Ejlert Løvborg's been taken to hospital. He . . . won't last long.

MRS ELVSTED (*screaming*). Oh God, God.

TESMAN. Hospital? Not long?

HEDDA (*blurting it*). So soon?

MRS ELVSTED (*wailing*). Oh Hedda, we parted in anger.

HEDDA (*aside to her*). Thea!

MRS ELVSTED (*not noticing*). I must go to him. I must see him before he dies.

BRACK. Mrs Elvsted, impossible. They won't allow visitors.

MRS ELVSTED. At least tell me what happened.

TESMAN. He hasn't . . . hurt himself? Has he?

HEDDA. I'm sure he has.

TESMAN. Hedda, how can you know?

BRACK (*giving her a straight look*). Unfortunately, Mrs Tesman, you've guessed quite right.

MRS ELVSTED. No!

TESMAN. Hurt himself.

HEDDA. Shot himself.

BRACK. Right again, Mrs Tesman.

MRS ELVSTED (*fighting for self-control*). Your Honour, when did it happen?

BRACK. This afternoon. Between three and four.

TESMAN. Good Heavens! Where?

BRACK (*after a slight hesitation*). My dear man, at his lodgings.

MRS ELVSTED. That can't be right. I was there myself between six and seven.

BRACK. Somewhere else, then. I don't know exactly. All I know is that someone found him. Shot. In the chest.

MRS ELVSTED. How dreadful. That he should die like this.

HEDDA (*to* BRACK). In the chest? You're sure?

BRACK. Certain.

HEDDA. Not the temple?

BRACK. The chest, Mrs Tesman.

HEDDA. Well . . . the chest will do.

BRACK. Pardon?

HEDDA (*evasively*). Nothing.

TESMAN. And the wound was serious, you say?

BRACK. Beyond cure. He's probably . . . gone already.

MRS ELVSTED. He has! I know it. Gone! Oh Hedda . . .

TESMAN. But who told you all this?

BRACK (*curtly*). The police. I had . . . business there.

HEDDA (*loud*). At last, success.

TESMAN (*horrified*). Hedda! Whatever d'you mean?

HEDDA. I mean that this is beautiful.

BRACK. Mrs Tesman . . .

TESMAN. Beautiful?

HEDDA. Ejlert Løvborg has closed his account with himself. Had the courage to do . . . what had to be done.

MRS ELVSTED. It's not true. Not this. A moment of madness.

TESMAN. Despair.

HEDDA. I'm sure it wasn't.

MRS ELVSTED. It must have been. Despair. Like when he tore our book to pieces.

BRACK (*astonished*). Your book? The manuscript? He tore it up?

MRS ELVSTED. Last night.

TESMAN (*whispering*). Hedda, we'll never get out of this.

BRACK. What an odd thing to do.

TESMAN (*pacing*). Fancy Ejlert, leaving the world like this. Not even leaving behind the book that would make him immortal.

MRS ELVSTED. If it could only be reconstructed.

TESMAN. Reconstructed. Oh if only –

MRS ELVSTED. Dr Tesman, perhaps it can.

TESMAN. What d'you mean?

MRS ELVSTED (*going through her bag*). Look. I've still got his notes. The ones he dictated from.

HEDDA (*closer*). Oh.

TESMAN. Mrs Elvsted! You kept them!

MRS ELVSTED. They're here. I brought them when I came to town. They've been in my bag ever since.

TESMAN. Let me see them.

MRS ELVSTED *hands him a sheaf of notes.*

MRS ELVSTED. They're out of order. All mixed up.

TESMAN. Still we might be able to . . . If we helped each other . . .

MRS ELVSTED. Oh, do let's try. Let's try.

TESMAN. We'll succeed. We must! I'll devote my life to it.

HEDDA. Jørgen? Your life?

TESMAN. Well, as much as I can spare. My own work can wait. D'you see, Hedda? I must. I owe it to Ejlert's memory.

HEDDA. Perhaps you do.

TESMAN. Mrs Elvsted, we must take ourselves in hand. No use brooding on the past. We must clear our minds –

MRS ELVSTED. Doctor Tesman, I'll try. I'll try.

TESMAN. Come on then. We'll start right away. Where shall we work? In here? No: in there. Excuse me, Brack. This way, Mrs Elvsted. This way.

MRS ELVSTED. Please God it works!

She and TESMAN go into the inner room. She takes off her coat and hat. They sit at the table under the lamp and begin a feverish examination of the papers. HEDDA sits in the armchair by the stove. After a moment, BRACK goes beside her.

HEDDA (*murmured*). Freedom, Your Honour. That's what it means, this Løvborg business. Freedom.

BRACK. He's certainly set free.

HEDDA. Freedom for me, I mean. I'm free, because I know it's still possible to choose. Freewill! Still possible, and beautiful.

BRACK (*with a smile*). Ah, Mrs Tesman –

HEDDA. I know what you're going to say. You're a kind of expert too. A kind of . . . Well.

BRACK (*looking intently at her*). Ejlert Løvborg was more important to you than you like to admit, even to yourself. Or am I mistaken?

HEDDA. I can't answer that. All I know is that Ejlert Løvborg had the courage to choose the kind of life he wanted to lead. And now this, this triumph, this beautiful deed. He had the strength, the will, to tear himself away from the banquet of life . . . so early.

BRACK. It's a charming fantasy, Mrs Tesman, and I'm sorry to shatter it –

HEDDA. Fantasy?

BRACK. It would've been shattered anyway, quite soon.

HEDDA. What d'you mean?

BRACK. He didn't . . . choose to shoot himself.

HEDDA. I don't understand.

BRACK. Things weren't exactly as I described.

HEDDA (*tense*). Something else?

BRACK. For poor Mrs Elvsted's sake, I kept a few details back.

HEDDA. What details?

BRACK. First: he's dead already.

HEDDA. In the hospital?

BRACK. Without regaining consciousness.

HEDDA. Anything else?

BRACK. His . . . accident . . . wasn't at his lodgings.

HEDDA. Not important.

BRACK. Maybe not. I'll tell you. They found him, shot, in Mamzelle Diana's boudoir.

HEDDA *starts up, then falls back.*

HEDDA. Not today, Your Honour! He can't have gone back there today.

BRACK. This afternoon. He was looking for something they'd taken from him. He was raving: a lost child -

HEDDA. And that's . . .

BRACK. I wondered if he meant his manuscript. But now I hear that he tore it up himself. It must have been his wallet.

HEDDA. So that's where they found him.

BRACK. With a pistol in his breast pocket. It had been fired. It had wounded him fatally.

HEDDA. Yes, in the chest.

BRACK. In the . . . lower parts.

HEDDA (*looking up at him in disgust*). Even that! Mean, sordid, like everything else I touch.

BRACK. Mrs Tesman, there's something else. Just as sordid.

HEDDA. What?

BRACK. The pistol –

HEDDA (*holding her breath*). What about it?

BRACK. He must have stolen it.

HEDDA (*jumping up*). Stolen it! No! He didn't!

BRACK. It's the only explanation. He must have stolen it. Sh!

TESMAN *and* MRS ELVSTED *come in from the inner room.* TESMAN *has both hands full of papers.*

TESMAN. It's no use, Hedda. I can't see a thing under that lamp. Not a thing.

HEDDA. You can't see a thing.

TESMAN. Could we sit in here for a while, perhaps, at your writing-table?

HEDDA. Of course. (*Quickly.*) Just a moment. I'll tidy it first.

TESMAN. No need. There's plenty of room.

HEDDA. No, no, I'll clear it. All this can go on the piano. There.

She has taken something from the bookshelf, covered with sheet music. She puts some more music on top of it and carries the whole armful through to the inner room. TESMAN puts his papers on the table, and fetches the lamp from the corner table. He and MRS ELVSTED sit down and begin work again. HEDDA comes back, and stands behind MRS ELVSTED's chair, gently stroking the woman's hair.

Any progress, Thea? With the Ejlert Løvborg memorial?

MRS ELVSTED (*looking up disconsolately*). It's going to be very hard.

TESMAN. We've got to try. It's essential. Sorting out someone else's papers – I know about that.

HEDDA *sits on one of the stools by the stove.* BRACK *stands over her, leaning on the armchair.*

HEDDA (*in a low voice*). What were you saying about the gun?

BRACK (*low*). He must have stolen it.

HEDDA. Why stolen?

BRACK. There's no other explanation, Mrs Tesman.

HEDDA. Oh.

BRACK (*looking at her*). He came here this morning. Didn't he?

HEDDA. Yes.

BRACK. You were alone with him?

HEDDA. For a while.

BRACK. While he was here, did you leave the room at all?

HEDDA. No.

BRACK. Think. Not even for a moment?

HEDDA. Perhaps a moment, into the hall.

BRACK. Where did you keep your pistol-case?

HEDDA. I . . . well, on the –

BRACK. Mrs Tesman, where?

HEDDA. There, on the writing-desk.

BRACK. Have you checked it since, to see if both pistols are there?

HEDDA. No.

BRACK. No need. I saw the pistol on Løvborg's body. I recognised it at once, from yesterday. And from before.

HEDDA. Did you bring it?

BRACK. It's with the police.

HEDDA. What will they do?

BRACK. Try to trace the owner.

HEDDA. D'you think they'll succeed?

BRACK (*bending over her, whispering*). No, Hedda Gabler. So long as I hold my tongue.

HEDDA (*looking sideways at him*). And if you don't?

BRACK (*shrugs*). You could still say it was stolen.

HEDDA (*firmly*). Rather death!

BACK (*with a smile*). People say that. No one does it.

HEDDA (*not answering*). Suppose the pistol wasn't stolen. And the owner was traced. What then?

BRACK. Mrs Tesman: scandal.

HEDDA. Scandal!

BRACK. The one thing you're afraid of. You'd have to appear in court, of course. You and Mamzelle Diana. She'd have to explain how it happened. Was it accident . . . murder? Did he reach for the pistol to threaten her, and shoot himself? Did she snatch it from him, shoot him and put it back in his pocket? She could have done that. She's a strong young woman, Mamzelle Diana.

HEDDA. These sordid details have nothing to do with me.

BRACK. But you'll have to explain why you gave him the gun in the first place. And what possible conclusion d'you think they'll draw from what you say?

HEDDA (*lowering her head*). I never thought of that.

BRACK. Luckily there's no danger, so long as I hold my tongue.

HEDDA (*looking up at him*). You mean I'm in your power, Judge Brack. You . . . own me.

BRACK (*low whisper*). Hedda, darling, trust me. I won't take advantage.

HEDDA. I'm still in your power. At your disposal. A slave.

She gets up impatiently.

I won't have it. I won't.

BRACK (*with a half-mocking glance*). You will. What can't be cured . . .

HEDDA (*returning his glance*). We'll see.

She goes to the writing-desk. Hiding a smile, and imitating TESMAN's *way of speaking, she says:*

Well now, Jørgen, how does it look? Eh? Look?

TESMAN. Heaven knows, Hedda. There's months of work, that's for sure.

HEDDA (*as before*). Months of work.

She strokes MRS ELVSTED's *hair.*

How marvellous for you, Thea. To sit here with Tesman – as once you sat with Ejlert Løvborg.

MRS ELVSTED. If I could only inspire your husband too.

HEDDA. You will, in time.

TESMAN. Already, Hedda. Already. I think so. You go and talk to His Honour.

HEDDA. You don't need me here, either of you?

TESMAN. There's nothing you can do. Nothing at all. (*Turning his head.*) Brack, you don't mind keeping Hedda company?

BRACK (*glancing at* HEDDA). My pleasure.

HEDDA. Thank you. But I'm feeling rather tired. I'll lie down a moment, in there on the sofa.

TESMAN. Do that, darling. Yes.

HEDDA goes into the inner room and draws the curtains behind her. After a moment, we hear her playing wild dance-music on the piano. MRS ELVSTED *jumps up.*

MRS ELVSTED. Oh! What's that?

TESMAN runs to the entrance.

TESMAN. Not tonight, darling! Think of Aunt Rina. Not to mention Ejlert.

HEDDA (*looking through the gap in the curtains*). Not to mention Aunt Julia. All of them. I won't make a sound.

She draws the curtains closed behind her.

TESMAN (*at the writing-desk*). She's upset to see us at such a tragic task. Mrs Elvsted, I tell you what: why don't you move in with Aunt Julia? I'll come round every evening. We'll sit and work there. Work there!

MRS ELVSTED. It might be best –

HEDDA (*from the inner room*). I hear what you're saying, Tesman. And what will I do, every evening, here?

TESMAN (*turning over the papers*). I'm sure His Honour will be kind enough to call.

BRACK (*calling cheerfully from the armchair*). Mrs Tesman, every evening! We'll have such a jolly time . . .

HEDDA (*clearly and audibly*). You really hope so, Judge Brack. Cock of the walk –

We hear a shot, inside. TESMAN, MRS ELVSTED *and* BRACK *jump to their feet.*

TESMAN. She's playing with those guns again.

He pulls the curtains and runs in, followed by MRS ELVSTED. HEDDA *is lying dead on the sofa. Noise and confusion. Enter* BERTA *right, beside herself.* TESMAN *shrieks at* BRACK.

Shot herself! In the temple! Shot herself!

BRACK (*slumping in the chair*). No one does that. No one.

End of the play.